Management & Strategy

By

Raushan Gross

Management & Strategy
Copyright © 2021 by North American Business Press, Inc
ISBN: 978-1-948915-19-9

NORTH
AMERICAN BUSINESS
P R E S S

North American Business Press
Atlanta, Georgia
Miami, Florida
New York, New York,
Toronto, Canada

First Printing, 2021

To Minnie, Bear, and Wendy, with love

The Kitchen Table

Contents

Preface

This book is a collection of chapters on management topics ranging from the firm's flexibility to leadership, followership, and strategy. Each chapter suggests new ways of viewing the firm within the context of a new economy. The new economy calls for the firm to consider integrating flexibility, leadership, followership, and organizational strategy in the workings of a dynamic economic landscape.

Because this is a collection of theoretical considerations related to management and dynamic organizational theory in the current economic climate. New economic climates beg for new economic thinking and strategic responses to economic trends, forces, and circumstances. This book explores the fundamental managerial literature under a new light that serves to engage fresh questions about the nature of management, leadership, and followership. In this regard, the reader will notice a consistent dynamic theme of managerial adaptiveness to dynamic economic imperatives.

Thoughts from some of the most prominent authors in management, leadership, economics, and firm theories are found in this book. The proceeding chapters construct the literature into a relevant whole so that the insights might transmute it into application. I wrote this book to set forth on the new frontiers of management and the firm, if there are any, within the fundamental frameworks of management, economics, strategy, and leadership. As a result of constructing these areas for a new reality, I include theoretical approaches for future research opportunities.

Raushan Gross, Ph.D.

Chapter 1:
The Constrained and Unconstrained Strategist

With many views of the firm (e.g., resource-based, knowledge-based, strategy-based, and entrepreneurial), there has been little if any discussion regarding the constrained and unconstrained views of strategists and their view of the firm. A firm's strategic leaders operate with either a constrained or unconstrained view. Strategic leadership requires a commitment from the leadership ranks (e.g., upper echelon) to acquire resources, invest in human and social capital, and endure psychological risks. Strategic leaders' view of the firm ultimately directs strategies and business models with either flexibility or rigidity.

These two contrasting views of the strategist, regardless of their perceived merits or demerits, can have advantageous or devastating effects on strategy and market positioning in the long and short run. This chapter extensively describes constrained and unconstrained strategists and their view of the firm under the auspices of market uncertainty. The goal is to build a theory for academics and provide insight for the practicing strategist.

INTRODUCTION

Management and strategy theorists have often explained the actions of the firm without considering the strategist's vision and his or her impact on a firm's strategic type, flexibility, approach, and market decision or trajectory. Mintzberg and Waters (1985) made a salient theoretical construction that parallels the purpose of the current study: a strategy "walks on two feet, one deliberate, the other emergent" (p. 271). To date, management and strategy theories need a category of strategists to illuminate the differences between a *constrained strategist* and an *unconstrained strategist*. Their vision and ideological tremendously impact the flexibility and or direction of the firm.

With this dichotomy between a constrained and an unconstrained strategist, the current study attempts to develop a theory that provides insight into those who create, control, direct, and lead strategic initiatives in the firm. To date, there have been proponents of the resource-based view of the firm (Barney, 1991; Wernerfelt, 1984), knowledge-based theory of the firm (Grant, 1996; Sveiby, 2001), entrepreneurship of resource-based theory (Alvarez & Busenitz, 2001), and strategy theory of the firm (Phelan & Lewin, 2000). However, strategic management theory does not acknowledge the implicit views of strategic choices and types that manifest through a strategist's view.

It is theorized that it is the strategist's view, perceptions, vision, assumptions, and values that underlie his or her view of the firm that impact the firm's strategy. Categorization of the strategist's decision-making, interpretation, vision, and view as affecting the firm's implicit or explicit trajectory has been implied but never elaborated in the strategic approach and decision-making of the firm in the long-standing management and strategic literature (Miller, Kets de Vries, & Toulouse, 1982; Miller & Toulouse, 1986; Mintzberg, 1973; Peterson, Smith, Martorana, & Owens, 2003).

Mintzberg and Waters (1985) and McCarthy (2003) referenced novel actions derived from management as being entrepreneurial. Giberson et al. (2009) referred to entrepreneurial managers as similar to charismatic leaders. If we fast forward, firms now call for a continuous increase in performance, requiring all levels of the firm to be innovative and entrepreneurial. This current chapter addresses how to dichotomize strategists based on their explicit or implicit vision related to the firm's strategic risk tolerance. Strategists might be entrepreneurial, but if their risk tolerance is low, they are under a constrained view of the firm's direction and pursue constrained actions. Mintzberg and Waters asked, "How do organizations make important decisions and link them together to form strategies?" (p. 44). Can these views assist in understanding the nature of strategic flexibility or risk-averse behaviors? The current study's objective is to define, frame, and place into context a nascent theory called the *constrained and unconstrained strategists' view of the firm.*

The current research uses strategic leadership, upper echelon theory, and enterprise flexibility as theoretical bases for developing a conception of a strategist's view and its implications on a firm's strategic approach. Mintzberg and Waters (1985) saliently provided seven types of strategies to use as reference: planned, entrepreneurial, ideological, umbrella, process, unconnected, and imposed. While Mintzberg and Waters described the types of strategies, they did not dichotomize the views that distinguish strategists.

For example, if a firm's leadership approaches a strategy type—be it planned, imposed, ideological, or entrepreneurial—do the strategists already have a preconceived view? Does their constrained or unconstrained view inform their choice of strategy type, direction, resource allocation, and/or market trajectory? The constrained and unconstrained views of firm theory inform and build on the strategy types developed by the conceptualization of enterprise flexibility by Mintzberg and Waters, Volberda (1999) and Sharma and Jain (2010).

The current study primarily seeks to propose that strategists possess a basic *view of the firm* that is dichotomized as either constrained or unconstrained and influences the firm's strategic decisions and direction (Mintzberg, 1987). The importance of this chapter is to envelop the importance of a CEO's vision and view of the firm as a driver of "conception preceding action" (Mintzberg, 1978, p. 11). Alternatively, as McCarthy (2003) described strategy, it is activities that entail doing things creatively and competitively. With that, this chapter attempts to link strategic leadership with constrained and unconstrained views of the firm in the contexts of uncertainty and competitive business environments (Barbuto, 2016).

Perhaps a strategist's flexibility or rigidity mirrors the ideology and sentiments of the firm's strategic leadership. Hypothetically, if an unforeseen opportunity emerges, what action seems likely to take shape based on the strategist's view of the firm? These propositions are not an attempt to de-emphasize the merits or demerits of a strategic planning process; many (Barbuto, 2016; Mintzberg, 1994) have understood the planning process as an indispensable method that educates, explains, and directs the external resources needed to pursue market-based action—*ad hoc* or otherwise.

Strategic planning derives from a strategic reference point (Fiegenbaum, Hart, & Schendel, 1996) that affects the organizational view/vision of strategy relative to risk aversion, risk-seeking, or risk tolerance behaviors; these risk factors are conceptualizations that affect future strategy types and directions of the enterprise. McCarthy (2003) pointed out that some managers have more or less risk tolerance than others, and the same rule applies to risk-averse managers. Strategic leadership serves as a critical component of the strategy development process, namely, as the primary driver of human capital and the firm's cognitive molder of future-oriented action. Changes in market dynamics directly and/or indirectly impact a firm's strategic flexibility and strategic choices (Volberda, 1999). Strategic leaders' strict adherence or lack thereof to their firm's mission and use of resources is the corollary to the inevitable conflict of missions, visions, and the positive consequences of strategic flexibility, malleability, and adaptability between members of the upper echelon. The dearth of literature linking strategic leadership and enterprise flexibility from the strategists' view of the firm elicits more attention both theoretically and practically.

The connection between strategic leadership and enterprise was flexibly alluded to by McCarthy (2003), who presupposed that power, personality, crises, and life cycle changes inevitably produce strategy formulation. To add, in their landmark study, Mintzberg and Waters (1985) stated, "We have not as yet studied an organization dominated by an ideology" (p. 262). As long as there are differences between leaders' ideals and philosophies, direction, power structure, use of resources, and strategy type, there arises a conflict of visions (Sowell, 2007). This conflict in ideologies has an implicit and explicit impact on future strategic approaches, strategic choices, and views of the firm. These conflicts of vision initiate from the upper echelon strategists themselves. The two types of strategists—constrained and unconstrained—their approaches to strategy formulation and differences in views have real implications for the firm.

The first motivating factor of this study is derived from Sharma and Jain's (2010) contention that there is a gap in strategic flexibility literature concerning the role of strategic leadership as the primary driver of firm-level performance and strategic trajectory. The reason for such a gap relates to leadership (i.e., style, thinking, and vision), which remains one of the least recognized areas in the managerial and flexibility literature (Malewska & Sajdak, 2014; Volberda, 1999). Suppose leadership is a major driving force on the capacity for strategic flexibility. In that case, the culture (i.e., barriers and resistance to flexibility) can hinder or cultivate the capacity for flexibility (Trice & Beyer, 1993) if it has the support of upper echelon and subordinates (Giberson et al., 2009; Schein, 2004).

The second motivating factor of this chapter is to understand to what degree market signals influence strategists' decision to either optimize or maximize the firm's resources based on the interpretations of market signals and how they take either a *constrained* or *unconstrained* view of the firm.

Upper echelon theory, enterprise flexibility, and strategic leadership are woven together to form a tapestry of interconnected linkages that create a theory of the constrained or unconstrained view of the firm. The literature review offers insights on strategic leadership, constrained and unconstrained views, a theoretical framework, discussion and propositions, and a conclusion. Together this chapter describes and operationalizes constrained and unconstrained strategists and their view of the firm. The literature reveals a careful examination and explication for further theoretical development.

LITERATURE REVIEW

The top management team operates as the intellectual hub of the firm with their primary role to craft tactics that need foresight to adopt changes in response to new business environments (Eggers & Kaplan, 2009). The strategist's reasoning develops through education, experiences, knowledge acquisition, functional role, age, and leadership abilities. Top managers make strategic trade-offs based on education, role, and experience, even more so in uncertain business environments, using intellectual abilities (Buyl, Boone, & Matthyssens, 2011). These intellectual abilities and personal qualities are important when thinking strategically (Finkelstein, 1992) and making strategic decisions (Miller & Droge, 1986) in general.

Consider top management members who value change are most often those who initiate change when dissatisfied with the status quo. Henceforth, upper-echelon perspectives on change significantly impact whether deductive or inductive initiation of the change in strategy is executed within a firm (Mintzberg & Waters, 1985). Change, change performance, and dealing with uncertainty are not viewed the same across management. Finkelstein (1992) proclaimed that CEOs' cognitive abilities and personality act as powerful vehicles to transform the firm and increase performance outcomes during uncertain times (Waldman, Javidan, & Varella, 2004).

The Strategic Leadership View of the Firm
Kamila and Sajdak (2014) defined strategic leadership as "the ability to combine visionary operational management and the ability

to connect ideas in company operations while taking into account their limitations" (p. 145). Grzesik (2011) explained strategic leadership as the ability to cope with situations that are difficult to predict, unmanageable, and often without clear paths to improvement during turbulent times and in competitive environments.

Strategic leadership focuses on the organization-wide mobilization of resources. At the individual level, strategic leaders mobilize resources by awakening, envisioning, and re-architecting processes, people, and parameters. Tichy and Sherman (1993) asserted that strategic leaders are creators and maintainers of culture and climate. One of the most salient traits of strategic leaders is their ability to provide a vision and convert their vision to action, realized or manifested, in-market tactics. Mintzberg (1987) said, "Strategy is consistency in behavior, whether or not intended" (p. 12).

This implies that cognition, personality, and the ability to identify market opportunities are encased in the strategist's reference point of the firm's marketplace position relative to competitors. Strategic leaders are well informed, share foresight, and think strategically about processes of reformulation and recombination of the firm's resources. Strategic leaders reframe situations directly or indirectly related to foreseen or unforeseen changes because landscape changes serendipitously morph into emerging realities. Change in the competitive landscape invokes a level of uncertainty in strategic leadership commitment to preexisting business plans, often unaligned with pre-planned courses of action based on preexisting reference points.

Strategic leadership has the unique role of shaping the input and implementation of the firm's values and strategic flexibility. The strategic leadership's reference point and nature of risk tolerance or flexibility influence their view of the firm, causing them to either push the envelope (i.e., Steve Jobs' return to Apple) or refocus on core competencies, causing a decrease in innovation and concerns on application (i.e., Lou Gerstner at IBM; Montgomery, 2008). Table 1 displays the links between strategic leadership attributes/characteristics and a firm's strategy.

Table 1

Strategic Leadership Attributes' Linkage to the Firm's Vision

Strategic Leadership Attributes	Firm's Vision
Thinking strategically to create combinations and recombinations of resources or units toward a future vision	Unconstrained
Connecting current visions with a historical perspective	Constrained
Transforming a future-oriented vision combined with the firm's historical vision	Unconstrained
Consolidating strategic activities to realign with the firm's preexisting vision	Constrained

Constrained View of Strategy

The constrained view of strategy emphasizes and adheres to the planning process as a mechanism to defend competitive advantages. This view is in line with the classical theory of management (March & Simon, 1958; Mintzberg & Waters, 1985; Parsons, 1960; Weber, 1958). Despite market signals in the face of known competitive pressures, constrained strategists remain constant in the face of serendipitous occurrences. A constrained ideology shapes the strategic direction and operates under a set of assumptions: well-defined tactics, intent farsightedness, limited acknowledgment of market forces, and risk averse in strategic tactics and positioning.

Under a constrained view, the foci are narrowly goal-oriented as they correspondingly relate to limited strategic choices. For example, Kodak's leadership pursued a narrow focus on film while all along receiving market signals that the industry was moving in a different direction (Larish, 2012). It appears that Kodak's leadership had a constrained view of strategy. Kodak's constrained strategy was evidenced by their sluggish transition from film to digital compared to their competitors and industry changes.

Very little of the constrained strategy's intricacies are altered, especially if the firm enjoys a competitive position in an existing market. Constrained strategists view structure as preceding strategy in every way possible, which creates internally cultivated strategic myopia and a moderate waste of resources due to misapplied absorptive capacity. The constrained strategist's aversion to becoming a first-mover remains high—but only if, however, these risk tactics come from within the firm's strict and narrow purview.

Constrained strategic leaders acknowledge that differentiation and change come at a cost (Porter, 1985). If differentiation is needed for growth, then idea generation starts with historical data to justify future decision-making. Constrained strategists are bound by historical indicators and trends and tradition to a larger degree than *unconstrained* strategists. For example, before constrained strategists contemplate how to capture technological value, they first analyze its historical adaptiveness related to organizational and structural adsorption rates. The constrained strategist perceives employee behavior as fixed and unmalleable. A technological value that proves to work with respect to the level of complexity, risk potential, and governance peculiarities more than likely will be examined for further analysis based on risk tolerance. A constrained strategist asks *how* before implementing innovation.

The constrained strategist seeks to eliminate innovative behavior and flexibility as much as possible—inventiveness and serendipity are valued alternatively by the constrained strategist. The constrained view of innovative behavior first views the costs of idea failures because best practices and policies previously determined (i.e., in times of certainty and uncertainty) guide the strategic trajectory. Policies and actions are established by data—data precede action and data drive action. Strategic action, adaptive or otherwise, needs not precede data even when market signals are strong and apparent. Constrained strategists operate within the framework of logical incrementalism and optimizing resources to capture value through precise planning—to a much lesser extent capturing value via the entrepreneurial spirit. This value capturing and optimizing purview of constrained strategists comes from an inherent aversion to maximizing resources. Because of the long-term consequences of maximization, precedents are heavily considered before commitments regarding resource allocations are made.

Constrained View of the Firm: Optimization in the Face of Uncertainty

Despite unforeseen circumstances and competitive signals to operate under a change of business model, the constrained strategist interprets market signals as the need to optimize preexisting resources, industry position, supplier relationship, or even strategic business units. While value proposition and profit are as much a consideration with any strategist (or strategic team), the constrained view of strategy focuses on vertical value creation—vertical value only created from within and not from an outside-in perspective. For this reason, these strategists are constrained as to the use and limits of resources when existing industries and markets are uncertain.

Coordination of resources, human or otherwise, is transmuted more so either through a directional strategy—stability or retrenchment and/or parent growth strategy in terms of attaining profit. For example, de Sola Pool (1977) reminded us that during the years 1877-1878, William Orton, president of Western Union, turned down the opportunity to purchase the Bell Venture Telephone (AT&T/Ma Bell) patent and stayed within the purview of his aging markets and changing industry because he saw no real use in the "electrical toy" (p. 16). The least recognized constrained optimization is the detrimental realization of suboptimization that results from an internal myopic view of technology and resources in the face of uncertainty where, ultimately, a once-useful technology no longer unconstrains the firm's operations but rather, over time, constrains them.

Henry Havemeyer, nicknamed the *Sugar King*, once ruled the sugar industry but was faced with competition from an arch competitor in the coffee industry, John Arbuckle, owner of Arbuckle coffee (Cobb, 2017). Arbuckle's coffee company was one of the leading coffee manufacturers in the United States before the Civil War—one of the first to introduce roasting and packaging, differentiating them from other coffee producers (Cobb, 2017). At that time, the Sugar King was set on the diversification of products for his sugar manufacturing and refining firm. He made several attempts to compete in the coffee industry with Archbuckle by creating and applying flexible production methods. When the results were poor or indifferent to his view of the firm and the magnitude of flexibility, the Sugar King recoiled to his firm's core capability (i.e., sugar production) and remained constrained in attitude and action.

Unconstrained View of Strategy

The strategist with an unconstrained view tends to place extreme emphasis on wide-ranging and far-reaching external reference points as immediate targets. This view is akin to the postmodern ideal of management with an emphasis on a less rational approach to competitive forces and market position strategies (Covin & Wales, 2012; Haberstroh, Baring, & Mudgett, 1968; Miles, Snow, Meyer, & Coleman, 1978). This strategist embraces the tumult of strategic flexibility—strategic thinking and entrepreneurial spirit stay on the forefront of strategic actions. The basic axiom of an unconstrained view of the firm deems strategic flexibility a dynamic process—strategic efforts remain malleable to the point that products and service models change and readapt to market demands on an ad hoc basis. The firm's mission, of course, plays a major role and serves as the firm's anchor; however, interpretation of the mission underscores the *entrepreneurial spirit*. Supporting the entrepreneurial spirit is expected when change occurs and uncertainty is present; thus, processes are modified to respond to competitors' actions in the market and industry. Strategic thinking, in this case, is fluid throughout the firm because it increases absorptive capacity, which serves to expeditiously direct and/or redirect efficiency by tapping into slack resources.

Creative destruction, a term Joseph Schumpeter (1942) coined, explains the ethos of the unconstrained view in many ways. Schumpeter said the entrepreneurial spirit "comes from the new consumers, goods, the new methods of production or transportation, the new markets, the new forms of industrial organization" (p. 82). The unconstrained strategist embraces flexibility and embeds it into the firm's long-term strategy. Unconstrained strategists view slack resources as necessary to gain efficiency for tactical execution with the least amount of risk-averse behavior.

From the top-down, the ideology speaks to the spirit of creative destruction—arguably, a view that allows the firm to adjust and/or readjust performance levels to adapt to any type of change trajectory and adaptivity (i.e., prospectors, analyzers, defenders, and reactors). Based on the Miles and Snow (1978) taxonomy, the unconstrained strategist executes adaptive tactics either as *prospecting* and/or *analyzing*. The unconstrained strategist typifies the adaptive strategy in that the nature of the adaptive strategy maximizes opportunities and risks due to changes of the business landscape. The unconstrained strategist's view of vision, mission, effective leadership, and fiscal responsibility is not more or less fuzzy than the constrained strategist; rather, an unconstrained ideology pursues tactics, profit goals, and performance outcomes differently. It is an ideology that permeates one's interpretation of a business model, strategy direction, and optics in driving human capital.

Unconstrained View of the Firm: Maximization in the Face of Uncertainty

In the face of uncertainty, the unconstrained strategist supports growth as a process only in the sense of maximizing resources, market position, human capital, or otherwise. Directional and parent strategies are the standard as strategists gain synergy and create value. This strategist tends to maximize product and service offerings and innovative processes as they become realized. This strategist cultivates an internal climate that fosters the maximization of shareholder and stakeholder value and profitability. An unconstrained strategist emphasizes the importance of horizontal value creation—the value created from within the firm by using dynamic capabilities, human capital, and an inside-out vision of the firm.

The Dichotomy Between the Constrained and Unconstrained Views of the Firm

Strategic leaders possess either a constrained or unconstrained view of strategy based on several factors, including industry, experience, position, resources, intuition, and size of the firm. The flexibility of a strategy is gauged and measured by the strategist's view because the constrained strategist asks *how* and an unconstrained strategist asks *when*. Regardless of a strategy's flexibility or rigidity, the strategist's view is the main determinant of increasing or decreasing enterprise flexibility and internally creating value-added capabilities to sustain flexibility.

Watson (1963), founder of International Business Machines Corporation (IBM), displayed his strategic view and tolerance of flexibility embedded in his *basic beliefs*. Through his basic beliefs, Watson saw flexibility as an unavoidable risk. But at some point, in the firm's life cycle, depending on the market position, Watson knew a culture of beliefs and customs would necessitate a view to being incorporated in the longevity of his firm (constrained or unconstrained view) that was favorable in terms of the ability and capability to survive in the face of competitive forces. Watson's basic beliefs informed his unconstrained view of the firm: respect for the individual, best customer service, and the pursuit of happiness. Depending on the level of strategic flexibility initiated, the rate and absorption of resources significantly impact the mobilization of firm-level resources coupled with the firm's value-added activities.

In 2003, then IBM CEO, Sam Palmisano, held an unconstrained view of the firm's core values and strategically designed a 72-hour top-down meeting to openly discuss and reimagine IBM's core values. Roberts and Stockport (2009) pointed to the fact that Palmisano's IBM ValuesJam session was strategic flexibility at its best. Roberts and Stockport suggested that strategic flexibility and strategic choices available to the firm are related and determine the firm's ability to exploit these choices. Choice of strategy means a potential reorientation of an existing strategy, which implies that new ideas require new learning (Grzesik, 2011; Palmisano, 2004).

Strategic leaders primarily concern themselves with human capital, the combination or recombination of resources, connecting visions with a reality, and transforming visions during tumult and uncertainty. Because there are predictable and unpredictable strategic triggers that enable a firm's flexibility, the constrained view sees strategic enablers as only options to exercise if there is a transition between strategic phases or substantive market changes; even then, the enabling levers are not activated due to reaction from competitors. A constrained strategist seems likely to defend rather than prospect the frontier of a business landscape for changes or to create changes. Initiating strategic flexibility in an ad hoc climate is a natural, unconstrained methodology during the planning process. The unconstrained strategist cultivates a climate and spirit of innovative support so that the firm stays ahead of current external trends and changes identified as threats or opportunities (see Table 2).

Table 2

Distinctions Between Constrained and Unconstrained Strategists

Constrained Strategist	Unconstrained Strategist
Non-innovative	Innovative
Reactive	Responsive
Rigid	Flexible
Low tolerance for risks	Challenge risks (high tolerance)
Historically bound	Making/shaping history
Systems-oriented	Process-oriented
Closed system-oriented, rational decision-making style	Open system-oriented decision-making style
Value-free perspective	Value-laden perspective

DISCUSSION AND PROPOSITIONS

Table 1 depicts two divergent views of strategy—constrained and unconstrained. Both views acknowledge that strategy initiates at the upper echelon level before being driven by mid-level subordinates—the *modus operandi* of many firms. Typically, strategic views or attitudes encompass more than just one designated individual (the strategists) and often are supported through all levels of the firm (i.e., top management teams); therefore, both views (constrained and unconstrained) consider any strategy and business model development as a multi-actor function that accumulates multiple visions utilized to create activities to optimize and/or maximize performance, resources, and market position and to sustainably compete (Finkelstein, Hambrick, & Cannella, 2009; Kriger & Zhovobryukh, 2013; Yukl, 1989).

Additionally, Table 2 shows the strategic leadership concept as highly significant and associative with the strategist's constrained and or unconstrained view of the firm. Tables 1 and 2 explicitly shows that all ideas and future projections of the strategic direction starts with the strategist's view of the firm. The flexibility and/or trajectory of decisions extends to the firm from the outpouring of the strategist's view. To a degree, both types of strategists think strategically, plan combinations and recombinations, connect visions with reality, and transform visions to combine with the firm's mission.

This acknowledgment of a strategic leadership view of a firm provides insightful additions to theory and practical strategy development, mainly to determine the effects on strategy and strategy planning. Not to mention, this chapter closes the gap between the mainline characteristics of effective strategic leadership and strategic action. The dimensions, characteristics, and strategic leadership model explain their importance in shaping a firm's strategic trajectory. The likelihood that strategists engage in a sort of action in time of uncertainty is either constrained or unconstrained.

P1:   Strategic leaders' constrained view of the firm positively impacts the performance of the firm.

P2:   Strategic leaders' unconstrained view of the firm positively impacts the performance of the firm.

P3   Strategists with a constrained view lower the risk tolerance of the firm.

P₄   Strategists with an unconstrained view increase the risk
      tolerance of the firm.

CONCLUSION

Strategic leaders' view of the firm plays a vital role when they envisage strategic planning. Strategists' views impact the firm's strategic direction and create contention as operationalists vie for competing interests, which creates a conflict of visions (Sowell, 1987). This also influences strategists' views in such categories as the industry life cycle (temporal), firm life cycle (market position), and absorptive capacity (firm-level acquisition of critical knowledge). Even the notion of matching strategists to a strategic function leaves out the fundamental void that strategists possess an ideology that directly influences strategy itself and, if unnoticed, brings about either positive or negative operational results despite a perfect match.

Thus, strategic leadership involves making changes related to the direction of the firm, directly and indirectly, based on a long- or short-term vision, either individually or with members of the top management team whose role entails developing critical paths and formulating steps that implement vision into a strategy based on a constrained or unconstrained view of the firm. The notion that organizational flexibility does not require employee motivation is unfounded and nonsensical if looking through leadership and adapting to a change in circumstances. There is no conceivable way to achieve flexibility with unsatisfied employees who are demotivated to pursue their goals. Organizational flexibility is dynamic and pervasive in the sense that it requires people, processes, and managerial support to cultivate employees' capabilities to adjust and readjust to market demands, internal challenges, and innovative opportunities (Bran & Udrea, 2016) quickly and responsively.

Numerous types of organizational flexibility (technical, strategic, etc.) exist; however, whichever type is favored by the nature and multiplicity of diversity in various markets and then employed, there is a cause and a consequence of organizational flexibility. The unintended causes of flexibility are due to reactions that deviate from the status quo. The consequence is resistance to change and, ultimately, a reverberation to and from the initial change state—flexibility. When there is a change of state from one form to the next and back to the original form, flexibility has occurred. With that, the strategist's view accounts for changes in strategy without changes in value. The strategist accounts for changes in the values and becomes flexible, eventually reverting to an original state (i.e., the ratchet effect).

On net balance, the practical and theoretical need for a dichotomy between strategists' view of the firm is to place greater emphasis on the human side of making and direction strategy that might explain the antecedent of strategic outcomes. Therefore, these propositions need to be tested empirically to account for the inclination that, in fact, the constrained and unconstrained strategies are two categorizations that can explain how strategists' views of the firm might explain the outcomes of a firm's strategic trajectory in the marketplace.

REFERENCES

Alvarez, S. A., & Busenitz, L. W. (2001). The entrepreneurship of resource-based theory. *Journal of Management, 27*(6), 755-775.

Barbuto, J. E., Jr. (2016). How is strategy formed in organizations? A multi-disciplinary taxonomy of strategy-making approaches. *Journal of Behavioral and Applied Management, 3*(1), 822.

Barney, J. (1991). Firm resources and sustained competitive advantage. *Journal of Management, 17*(1), 99-120.

Bran, C., & Udrea, C. I. (2016). The influence of motivation and flexibility on job performance. *The European Proceedings of Social & Behavioural Sciences EpSBS, 15*, 135-143.

Buyl, T., Boone, C., & Matthyssens, P. (2011). Upper echelons research and managerial cognition. *Strategic Organization, 9*(3), 240-246.

Cobb, G. (2017). *The rise and fall of the Sugar King: A history of Williamsburg, Brooklyn 1844-1909.* Scotts Valley, CA: Independent Publishing Platform.

Covin, J. G., & Wales, W. J. (2012). The measurement of entrepreneurial orientation. *Entrepreneurship Theory and Practice, 36*(4), 677-702.

de Sola Pool, I. (1977). *The social impact of the telephone.* Cambridge, MA: MIT Press.

Eggers, J. P., & Kaplan, S. (2009). Cognition and renewal: Comparing CEO and organizational effects on incumbent adaptation to technical change. *Organization Science, 20*(2), 461-477.

Fiegenbaum, A., Hart, S., & Schendel, D. (1996). Strategic reference point theory. *Strategic Management Journal, 17*(3), 219-235.

Finkelstein, S. (1992). Power in top management teams: Dimensions, measurement, and validation. *Academy of Management Journal, 35*(3), 505-538.

Finkelstein, S., Hambrick, D. C., & Cannella, A. A. (2009). *Strategic leadership: Theory and research on executives, top management teams, and boards.* Oxford, UK: Oxford University Press.

Giberson, T. R., Resick, C. J., Dickson, M. W., Mitchelson, J. K., Randall, K. R., & Clark, M. A. (2009). Leadership and organizational culture: Linking CEO characteristics to cultural values. *Journal of Business and Psychology, 24*(2), 123-137.

Grant, R. M. (1996). Toward a knowledge-based theory of the firm. *Strategic Management Journal, 17*(S2), 109-122.

Grzesik, K. (2011). Identifying solutions in creating leader potential in an enterprise. *Journal of Positive Management, 2*(1), 25-36.

Haberstroh, C. J., Baring, J. A., & Mudgett, W. C. (1968). Organizing for product innovation. *IEEE Transactions on Engineering Management*, (1), 20-27.

Kriger, M., & Zhovtobryukh, Y. (2013). Rethinking strategic leadership: Stars, clans, teams, and networks. *Journal of Strategy and Management*, 6(4), 411-432.

Larish, J. J. (2012). *Out of focus: The story of how Kodak lost its direction*. CreateSpace Independent Publishers.

Malewska, K., & Sajdak, M. (2014). The intuitive manager and the concept of strategic leadership. *Management*, 18(2), 44-58.

March, J. G., & Simon, H. A. (1958). *Organizations*. Oxford, England: Wiley.

McCarthy, I. P. (2003). Technology management—A complex adaptive systems approach. *International Journal of Technology Management*, 25(8), 728-745.

Miller, D., & Droge, C. (1986). Psychological and traditional determinants of structure. *Administrative Science Quarterly*, 539-560.

Miller, D., Kets de Vries, M. F., & Toulouse, J. M. (1982). Top executive locus of control and its relationship to strategy-making, structure, and environment. *Academy of Management Journal*, 25(2), 237-253.

Miller, D., & Toulouse, J. M. (1986). Chief executive personality and corporate strategy and structure in small firms. *Management Science*, 32(11), 1389-1409.

Miles, R. E., Snow, C. C., Meyer, A. D., & Coleman, H. J., Jr. (1978). Organizational strategy, structure, and process. *Academy of Management Review*, 3(3), 546-562.

Mintzberg, H. (1973). Strategy-making in three modes. *California Management Review*, 16(2), 44-53.

Mintzberg, H. (1978). Patterns in strategy formation. *Management Science*, 24(9), 934-948.

Mintzberg, H. (1987). The strategy concept I: Five Ps for strategy. *California Management Review*, 30(1), 11-24.

Mintzberg, H. (1994). The fall and rise of strategic planning. *Harvard Business Review, 72*(1), 107-114.

Mintzberg, H., & Waters, J. A. (1985). Of strategies, deliberate and emergent. *Strategic Management Journal, 6*(3), 257-272.

Montgomery, C. A. (2008). Putting leadership back into strategy. *Harvard Business Review, 86*(1), 54.

Palmisano. (2004).

Parsons, T. (1960). *Structure and process in modern societies.* Glencoe, IL: Free Press.

Peterson, R. S., Smith, D. B., Martorana, P. V., & Owens, P. D. (2003). The impact of chief executive officer personality on top management team dynamics: One mechanism by which leadership affects organizational performance. *Journal of Applied Psychology, 88*(5), 795.

Phelan, S. E., & Lewin, P. (2000). Arriving at a strategic theory of the firm. *International Journal of Management Reviews, 2*(4), 305-323.

Porter, M. E. (1985). Technology and competitive advantage. *Journal of Business Strategy, 5*(3), 60-78.

Roberts, N., & Stockport, G. J. (2009). Defining strategic flexibility. *Global Journal of Flexible Systems Management, 10*(1), 27-32.

Schein, E. (2004). *Organizational culture and leadership* (3rd ed.). San Francisco, CA: Jossey-Bass.

Schumpeter, J. A. (1942). *Capitalism, socialism, and democracy.* New York, NY: Harper.

Sharma, M. K., & Jain, P. K. (2010). Revisiting flexibility in organizations: Exploring its impact on performance. *Global Journal of Flexible Systems Management, 11*(3), 51-68.

Sowell, T. (1987). *A conflict of visions: Ideological origins of political struggles.* New York, NY: Basic Books.

Sveiby, K. E. (2001). A knowledge-based theory of the firm to guide in strategy formulation. *Journal of Intellectual Capital, 2*(4), 344-358.

Tichy, N. M., & Sherman, S. (1993). *Control your destiny or someone else will: Lessons in mastering change—From the principles Jack Welch is using to revolutionize General Electric.* New York, NY: HarperCollins Publications.

Trice, H. M., & Beyer, J. M. (1993). *The cultures of work organizations*. Englewood Cliffs, NJ: Prentice-Hall.

Volberda, H. W. (1999). *Building the flexible firm: How to remain competitive*. New York, NY: Oxford University Press, USA.

Waldman, D. A., Javidan, M., & Varella, P. (2004). Charismatic leadership at the strategic level: A new application of upper echelons theory. *The Leadership Quarterly, 15*(3), 355-380.

Watson, T. J. (1963). The Ideas That Helped Build IBM. *New York, 95*, 97.

Watson, T. J. (1984). *Business and its beliefs*. New York, NY: McGraw-Hill.

Weber, M. (1958). *The Protestant ethic and the spirit of capitalism* (T. Parsons, Trans.). New York, NY: Scribner.

Wernerfelt, B. (1984). A resource-based view of the firm. *Strategic Management Journal, 5*(2), 171-180.

Yukl, G. (1989). Managerial leadership: A review of theory and research. *Journal of Management, 15*(2), 251-289.

Chapter 2:
Followership and Organizational Strategic Flexibility

What is the influence of followers in a firm that is challenged to adapt to serendipitous strategic market opportunities due to marketplace changes? What is the function of followers who are proxy to leadership during strategic flexibility at all levels of the firm?

This chapter presents a myopic integration of two theories— followership, and strategic flexibility—and integrates these theories in an attempt to envelop the role of followership and follower styles and ascertain if the consequences of followership negatively or positively impact strategic flexibility. In doing so, several of the main arteries of the followership theory are incorporated, and a microview of flexibility is developed as a cross-current. Four propositions are presented for further research in this ripe theoretical vineyard.

INTRODUCTION

As a starting point, the understanding of followership in the context of organizational strategic flexibility has not achieved maturity, and much of the literature on followership has been silent (Johnson, Lee, Saini, & Grohmann, 2003). Given the immense amount of authorship on leadership, there tends to be a forgotten element that is vital to the firm—followership. Effective leadership positively impacts firm performance; this is an axiom in much of the management and leadership literature to date. Followership theory, however, is still, for the most part, in its infancy. This might be due to the amount of emphasis on follower behaviors resultant of leadership. Most leadership literature focuses on leaders' characteristics and traits and not those of followers. This should come as no surprise based on the natural focal point on the consequences of leadership influences on followers' behaviors and output, especially within the organizational context (Yukl & Becker, 2006).

This chapter examines the potential influence of followership behaviors on the strategic flexibility of the firm. Understanding followership during strategic flexibility is timely for firms in high-velocity markets and industries. Uncertainty in the market economy, globalization, and intense competition for resources and consumers demand the firm to innovate via collaboration and to exercise flexible methods of strategy-making (Kim, 2018). Much of leadership and management theory implicitly assumes the role of followers as robotic, sheepish, and passive to the whims of leadership (Collinson, 2006). Plenty of attention has focused on enterprise flexibility, the entrepreneurial nature of the firm, entrepreneurial leadership, innovation, strategic thinking, and so forth. But there has been very little examination into the role of followership behaviors or styles as a function in strategic flexibility. It seems as if there is an invisible hand guiding the firm's valuable, imperfectly imitable, rare, and non-substitutable resources (Barney, 1991) to create a differentiated competitive advantage (Porter, 1985) and fuel an entrepreneurial spirit while promoting internal strategic flexibility that otherwise would not include the roles conducted by non-leaders.

The conceptual theories of strategic flexibility, management, and leadership effects are far from new (Johnson et al., 2003). The emergent nature of high-velocity firms intensifies the relationship of cooperation needed between leaders and followers due to the chaotic nature of change—strategic or otherwise. To a large extent, creative and imaginary ideas drive future strategic options that require a degree of collaborative thinking between followers and leaders (Bhardwaj & Momaya, 2006). This chapter explores the followership and flexibility content areas in a dialectic fashion to uncover the possible concatenation between two theories while setting up several propositions for future research. Rather than focusing on how leaders view followers' behaviors (Meindl, 1995) or how followers view their individual behaviors (Uhl-Bien & Pillai, 2007), this study questions if proxy followership behaviors influence the firm's ability to do things unintended from its projected market positioning. It is with urgent concern that an inquiry into the nature of followership and follower behaviors reconcile with those of the strategic actions of the firm, especially the change effects of the firm from a behavioral perspective (Carsten, Uhl-Bien, West, Patera, & McGregor, 2010).

The primary purpose of this study is to theoretically examine the interaction between followership and strategic flexibility. The secondary purpose is to ascertain the degree to which followership styles influence the three levels of strategic flexibility—organizational direction, organizational structure, and organizational operations. The proceeding sections of this chapter start with a brief and succinct literature review followed by a conceptual framework, discussion, and conclusion. This literature review serves to cull from the most salient literature in strategic flexibility and followership—the most significant work in the management, strategy, and leadership categories of authorship. In addition, the literature review provides a basis upon which a new conceptualization of followership is extended to strategic flexibility, *pari passu*.

LITERATURE REVIEW

Followership Models and Styles

Any given firm is likely to employ the capabilities of flexible individuals with the right to pursue tactics involved in the strategic flexibility process. Followership theory is one of the least observed areas in reporting the dynamic relationship between leadership and followership capabilities or, for that matter, most of the topics related to management and organizational studies. Furthermore, many theorists in the followership vineyard have made small connections between followership and leadership and followers' behavior as a result of the relationship with other dispositions and the climate of the firm. However, outside of the relational aspect, no theorists have postulated the impact of followership on other organizational variables at the firm level of analysis—such as strategic flexibility.

Because the firm on average has more followers than leaders (Collinson, 2006), it is ever more important to view followership through a contemporary lens—a theoretical lens that illuminates and disambiguates the notion of followership as typically conceived as one with a docile and sheepish disposition to one who is the knowledge purveyors and embodies collaborative dispositions. Within the often-complex relationships between leaders and followers during the organizational transition, change, and adaptation to market changes, followers act as the source of information to leadership, supporting a vital feedback loop (Oc & Bashshur, 2013). It is often thought that followers are a secondary factor in the dynamics of organizational leadership in that they are seemingly passive, weak performers who take orders without a sense of commitment and purpose. There is some evidence that followership and leadership are woven tightly together. Followers are highly effective in maintaining working relationships, offering constructive disruption, and playing the role of support in the various functions of the firm (Yukl & Becker, 2006). While change may be perceived as difficult, and flexibility perceived as expedient, flexibility and change differ in the sense that flexibility is a choice—

a choice to act or a choice to not act in any given external business environment. The consequences of strategic choices influence future market responses and flexibility in the use of the three pillars of firm-level analysis: direction, structure, and operation.

One of the first mentions of followership in the management literature was by Abraham Zalezink, who developed four follower types: impulsive subordinate, compulsive subordinate, masochistic subordinate, and withdrawn subordinate. Since that time, Kelley (1992) composed a set of followership styles: alienated, exemplary, passive, conformist, or pragmatist. Kelley structured the styles into four quadrants of followers who are active, passive, dependent, or independent. Similarly, Chaleff (2003) pioneered four followership styles to add to the preexisting follower models: implementer, partner, individualist, and resource. Finally, Kellerman (2008) added five followership types: isolated, bystander, participant, activists, and the diehard. Thinking about the role of followership means reimagining followers' behavior and their interaction with leadership. Followership is just as varied as leadership. There are styles, types, and motives that would explain why followers' interactions and roles may differ among individuals.

Followership and Organizational Leadership

A dynamic relationship characterizes the interaction between followers and leaders. Relationship starts with an initiation followed by a response, and responses can take on many forms and assume various patterns. Followers, unlike leaders, are individuals who hold either similar or dissimilar beliefs and attitudes and to varying degrees in the leader follower dynamic. Leaders are known to have a special role in *activating* the exchange between themselves and followers as roles change over time (Burns, 1978). In the same way, over time, followers articulate their wants and needs, which can change with increasing and continuous interaction with leadership.

Kelley (1992), one of the leading theorists in followership, advocates the theory and application of followership within organizational and political contexts. Two important outputs from a stream of followership behaviors are the styles patterned by followers. Kelly disambiguated the thinking of followers in two distinct ways: (a) Do they think for themselves? Are they independent critical thinkers? Or do they look to the leader to do the thinking for them? (b) Are they actively engaged in creating positive energy for the organization? Or is there negative energy or passive involvement?

Gardner (1990) expressed that the follower–leader dynamic depends on the time of crisis, prosperity, or recession and on the firm's ability to connect leaders and followers to a core purpose. Not all leaders are effective, and not all leaders can be most effective in every decision made. What are those skills and characteristics of followers in decision-making that result in strategic flexibility? Malakyan (2014) contended that followers influence leaders, and leaders influence followers. Followers' influence may take on a proxy or non-proxy function, but in any regard, followership does have a function in the speed and effectiveness of proxy decision-making with leadership and strategy development (Gross, 2019).

Kelley's (1992) archetypes of followership behaviors have been found to be related to leadership, individual performance, work output, job satisfaction, morale, and proxy entrepreneurial decision-making (Agho, 2009; Ehrhart & Klein, 2001). In fact, the leader and follower roles at times are presumably interchangeable because followers have to be leaders, and simultaneously, leaders play the roles of followers. If leadership and followership are conceptually disentangled from one another, then an environment of ineffective leadership would emerge. Agho (2009) showed that the expectations of leaders and followers were different in terms of who sets the overall tone, who takes the initiative, and the flow of communication between follower and leader.

Bjugstad, Thach, Thompso, and Morris (2006) expressed that a leader's effectiveness is dependent on the consent and observation of followers. Basically, without followers, there can be no leaders and vice versa. The relationships among followership, leadership, and the firm should be interrelated—in part due to the nature of the dynamic market competitiveness that ensues in the business landscape.

Competitors pose many threats to the firm's competitive advantages that simultaneously change the knowledge and information that guide strategic direction and the attainment of unforeseen market opportunities. Additionally, the basic approach to the workplace necessitates productive flexibility in order to combat the implicit forces of competitiveness (Ali & Camp, 2018). The synergies between followership and leadership can conceivably morph into an entrepreneurial spirit and shape the environment of the firm. The stronger the follower–leader dynamic, the more competitive a firm can be.

Strategic Flexibility

In *Toward the Next Economics and Other Essays*, Peter Drucker (2010) expressed the essence of strategic flexibility:

> But equally important, what technology is likely to become important and have an impact, and what technology either will fizzle out—like the "flying Model T"—or will have minimal social or economic impacts—like "automation"—is impossible to predict. (p. 54)

Strategic flexibility, as a resource capability of the firm, *nota bene,* is the application of resources to an immediate short-term need and contingent on adjustable follower behaviors as opposed to nonadjustable follower behaviors, regardless of whether the circumstances require short-term or long-run flexibility.

Strategic flexibility is certainly not a one-dimensional aspect of the firm. Rather, it is multidimensional, dynamic, and has a unique function within the firm. Strategic flexibility is dynamic because it permeates through many areas of the firm that relate to strategy and innovation (Combe, Rajala, Westerlund, & Möller, 2012; Ghorban & Gholipour, 2018); technology (Zhou & Wu, 2010); product output (Sanchez, 1995); competition, organizational capabilities (Kortmann, Gelhard, Zimmermann, & Piller, 2014); competitive advantage (Porter, 1985); and reversing ineffective decision-making (Shimizu & Hitt, 2004). Flexibility is the exercise of freedom of choice of firm direction in the tactical continuum in order to synthesize the dynamic interplay between the use of resources and emerging opportunities executed in an innovative manner with minimum time and effort. On the one hand, strategic flexibility is basically the ability to do something other than originally intended. In another sense, strategic flexibility is when a firm is able to adjust its objectives and use its acquired knowledge and capabilities toward a new emerging set of market objectives in the face of change.

Volberda (1996) explained that flexibility is the degree to which management has capabilities and can expeditiously activate them in the face of uncertainty. This leads to a primary research question: What, if any, is the role of followership in strategic flexibility, and what are the aspects of followership that enable or disable strategic flexibility within the firm? Promoting flexibility requires followers to be open to learning, creativity, and risk-taking to successfully adapt to emerging situations in the long term (Nanus, 1989).

A firm can pursue many types of strategies at any one point in time. It is not uncommon for firms to pursue multiple forms of strategies simultaneously. To determine which strategy is employed requires the observer not only to *hear* what is formally stated but also *see* what is being done—not to examine the immediate effects of strategic position but to consider the long-term consequences on the overall activities and directions of the firm, which is paramount in strategic flexibility. Observations at the firm level that a change in strategy is needed are related to a change of leadership, shifts in consumer taste and value scales, internal performance gaps, and invisible external forces. These factors can elicit a need to change to a flexible strategic trajectory. To switch between strategies due to emerging imperatives requires a change in orientation in light of the environmental and internal circumstances and internal responses to these external stimuli (Blumentritt & Danis, 2006). Strategic management behaviors are critical to the development and use of competitive capabilities (Schepers, Wetzels, & de Ruyter, 2005) that influence strategic choice.

Followership and leadership behaviors, capabilities, and *improvisational* activities aid in strategic flexibility (Blumentritt & Danis, 2006). In many ways, Sushil (2001) is one of the major forerunners in the flexibility domain. Sushil expressed that flexibility comprises the following dimensions: adaptiveness, openness, responsiveness, change, freedom, agility, reliance, and customization. There are six forms of flexibility: internal, external, organizational, strategic, marketing, and financial (Brozovic, 2018). Tactical execution in unrecognized, complex, unarranged, and unplanned environments requires strategic foresight and strategic thinking about a given reference point as a target. Gerwin (1993) agreed with Wadhwa and Rao (2002), suggesting there are many theoretical gaps in the concept of strategic flexibility. Strategic flexibility is a multidimensional construct defined as "the ability of the firms to respond and successively adapt to environmental change" (Combe & Greenley, 2004, p. 1458). Das (1995) described strategic flexibility as the capabilities of an organization to respond to market changes in the business landscape in a timely manner to combat competitive forces in the marketplace. These definitions of strategic flexibility speak of flexibility without reference to the strategists themselves and follower types, considering them almost as a nonfactor in strategic flexibility.

Wadhwa and Bhagwat (1998) explained that flexibility is not without a cost because any change in resource allocation from what perhaps is operating at an optimum level to a new critical path may cause those same resources to no longer work at optimal levels. Firm flexibility is a dynamic process and is pervasive in the sense that it necessitates action in areas that can increase followers' influence based on strategic effects on the firm's market position. If leadership ceases to influence the flow of flexibility, then mechanisms set in place will inherently decrease firm flexibility. Flexibility in every sense requires leadership in some aspect to influence response to first- or second-order change developments and market uncertainties (Bran & Udrea, 2016). However, not all types of followers are suited for strategic flexibility and change. For example, one type of follower may stand ready to accomplish a particular type of strategic action while another may not be ready to act. These differences in follower types and readiness are based on the description of the individual follower types—alienated, exemplary, passive, conformist, and pragmatist, or implementer, partner, individualist, and resource.

The Entrepreneurial Follower and Strategic Flexibility

Can entrepreneurial followers embody the entrepreneurial spirit needed to guide strategic flexibility? Many theorists have examined, tested, and hypothesized various aspects of entrepreneurial traits, the entrepreneurial leader, corporate innovation, and strategic entrepreneurial behaviors (Tseng & Tseng, 2019). Here is an attempt to connect followers' entrepreneurial spirit as a multiplier that affects the firm's strategic flexibility, which has yet to be discussed, measured, or even acknowledged in the extant literature as a strategic phenomenon.

In the spirit of identifying the follower's role in the entrepreneurial spirit, we are mostly concerned with how some followers might be more entrepreneurial than others based on Kelley's (1992), Chaleff's (2003), and Kellerman's (2008) conceptualizations of followers' styles. As such, numerous research articles have used the phrase *entrepreneurial spirit* without explication of the domains in which it is comprised. Internal entrepreneurship (i.e., corporate entrepreneurship) can be explained in four dimensions: new business venturing, innovations, self-renewal, and proactiveness (Bhardwaj & Momaya, 2006). Each of the corporate entrepreneurship dimensions implicitly involves the behaviors of followers and the leader's interaction in an effort to accomplish entrepreneurial goals. Leadership increases flexibility by empowering followers, being unafraid of change, feeling responsible for work tasks, delivering a speedy response, facilitating an open and honest culture, having a positive and determined attitude, sharing values, and continuously improving the customer-first orientation. A value framework exists between leaders and followers that must be congruent because shared values positively impact workplace commitment and job satisfaction (Krishnan, 2003), which relate to a positive impact on workplace roles and responsibilities and determines leadership influence strategies (Schepers et al., 2005).

Entrepreneurial Followership

The very idea that leadership has a role as an actor and as an entrepreneurial function in a market system has been proclaimed as one of the most important of any human action that can be applied in market phenomena. Entrepreneurial leaders are, for the most part, known to be major performance enhancers and innovators within any given firm. The main differences between individuals who are entrepreneurial and those who are not are drastic. Those who are not entrepreneurial cannot act in the marketplace due to an inability to adjust and maneuver either swiftly or flexibly through competitive conditions in the marketplace (Salerno, 2008).

In this sense, the entrepreneurial follower not only assumes a great deal of risk of capital employed to change conditions for their own sake but also for the satisfaction and desires of their customers and collaborators. What is dynamic here is that both entrepreneurial followers and entrepreneurial leaders seek ways to act in the market that reflect their purpose, skills, creativity, and ability to recombine resources based on external opportunities. How does entrepreneurial leadership as a concept work in practice with various follower types? How do these skills and market phenomena guide a firm through strategic flexibility? This can be partially explained with three categories of entrepreneurial followers—heterodox, orthodox, and unorthodox—based on the mode of flexibility and level of empowerment and proxy decision-making and interpretation of leadership vision and tasks in complex environments.

Three suppositions explain how the entrepreneurial spirit relates to strategic flexibility. First, the entrepreneurial spirit diffuses knowledge among the entrepreneurial group (i.e., the synergy of the entrepreneurial spirit converts from pockets of knowledge to open-source knowledge). Second, proxy followers are vital to the production of entrepreneurial endeavors (i.e., they are critical to the innovative climate and approach situations in various styles). Third, entrepreneurial followers add to the vitality (Kappel, 1960) of a firm and keep the firm supple because, most of the time, they are *close to the action* and can implement ideas and collect data from stem to stern. The spirit of innovation (Srivastava, Sultan, & Chashti, 2017) and the requisite competencies require changes related to the direction and differentiation of the firm that derive from the firm's knowledge base and previous decision-making outcomes. These decisions are made with leadership on entrepreneurial goals and unknown market forces. Strategic flexibility is motivated by the entrepreneurial spirit between strategic followers and strategic leadership, which creates coiling and recoiling (i.e., flexibility) to occur among strategic entrepreneurial activities that are often directed toward unknown market options.

DISCUSSION

Future research can take several paths to examine the propositions outlined in this chapter. Other things being equal, there are other effects worth looking into. How do followership styles fit into the corporate entrepreneurship dimensions? Are there particular capabilities that inspire effective followership? Is there a followership model to explain at a deeper level a few dimensions related to competitive advantages to the firm? Mintzberg (1989) suggested that firms must merge experts from different backgrounds and disciplines to gain effectiveness toward organizational goals. This statement is reassuring in that followership, within the context of team configurations, needs to be explored at the individual level of analysis and understood relative to the team goal and objective orientations.

CONCLUSION

The primary motivation of this theoretical study was to cull the relevant literature and to add to theory and integrate followership with the actions and activities of strategic flexibility within high-velocity firms. The following four propositions emerge from the literature:

P$_1$:   Followership in strategic flexibility either enables or disables strategic flexibility.

P2: Followership positively or negatively impacts the three levels of strategic flexibility (i.e., strategic direction, organizational structure, and organizational operations).

P3: Strategic flexibility increases by proxy entrepreneurial followers.

P4: Followership is positively related to competitive advantages in high-velocity firms.

Firms pursuing unintended strategic options require that both leaders and followers engage in an entrepreneurial spirit in order to reinvigorate the firm's defining paths or choice of path imitation (Chandler, 2001). Emerging or unintended strategic options require capabilities that both followers and leaders possess and that lead to innovative pursuits and changes in the firm's operations, structure, and strategy. Strategic followership behaviors are likely to be aligned with innovative approaches to the challenges firms face. This could result, for example, in designing new work-related goals to pursue client goals and market position or supporting functional demands and the subsequent recoiling that gets the firm's core capabilities back to their original position at any given time.

On the other hand, some followership behaviors may not be conducive to strategic flexibility or to what flexibility entails. Determining followership behaviors and/or follower styles should be the focus of future research, which is vital for understanding the operational and tactical nature of entrepreneurial followers in highly competitive markets, where competitive advantages and knowledge acquisition are paramount to a firm's success. Follower styles need to be explored more deeply, as has been attempted in this brief study. Further, it should be asked, is the follower–leader dynamic, when properly linked, able to create an environment of flexibility at all levels of the firm?

The entrepreneurial spirit is the underlying force that supports strategic flexibility (i.e., both tactical and operational) as a result of entrepreneurial followership. But there is more to ascertain relating to the mechanics of followership and the alignment between entrepreneurial followership and the willingness or unwillingness to change roles, change job duties or projects, join a different team, or share knowledge and expert functional dexterity to increase functional plasticity in competitive high-velocity markets. More needs to be elucidated as to the categories of entrepreneurial followers' styles that can be categorized as heterodox, orthodox, or unorthodox. These are questions not intended to be quixotic but applicable for firms that find inertia in the followership ranks that might otherwise negatively impact strategic flexibility.

REFERENCES

Agho, A. O. (2009). Perspectives of senior-level executives on effective followership and leadership. *Journal of Leadership & Organizational Studies, 16*(2), 159-166.

Ali, A. J., & Camp, R. C. (2018). Trends in the global marketplace and competitiveness: An observation. *Journal of Competitiveness Studies, 26*(3/4), 126-133.

Barney, J. (1991). Firm resources and sustained competitive advantage. *Journal of Management, 17*(1), 99-120.

Bhardwaj, B. R., & Momaya, K. (2006). Role of organizational flexibility for corporate entrepreneurship: Case study of FedEx Corporation. *Global Journal of Flexible Systems Management, 7*(1/2), 37-44.

Bjugstad, K., Thach, E. C., Thompson, K. J., & Morris, A. (2006). A fresh look at followership: A model for matching followership and leadership styles. *Journal of Behavioral and Applied Management, 7*(3), 304.

Blumentritt, T., & Danis, W. M. (2006). Business strategy types and innovative practices. *Journal of Managerial Issues, 18*(2), 274-291.

Bran, C., & Udrea, C. I. (2016). The influence of motivation and flexibility on job performance. *European Proceedings of Social & Behavioural Sciences, 15*, 135-143.

Brozovic, D. (2018). Strategic flexibility: A review of the literature. *International Journal of Management Reviews, 20*(1), 3-31.

Burns, J. M. G. (1978). *Leadership*. New York, NY: Harper & Row.

Carsten, M. K., Uhl-Bien, M., West, B. J., Patera, J. L., & McGregor, R. (2010). Exploring social constructions of followership: A qualitative study. *The Leadership Quarterly, 21*(3), 543-562.

Chaleff, I. (2003). *The courageous follower* (2nd ed.). San Francisco, CA: Berrett-Koehler. (Original work published 1995)

Chandler, A. D. (2001). *Inventing the electronic century: The epic story of the consumer electronics and computer industries.* New York, NY: Harvard University Press.

Collinson, D. (2006). Rethinking followership: A post-structuralist analysis of follower identities. *The Leadership Quarterly, 17*(2), 179-189.

Combe, I. A., & Greenley, G. E. (2004). Capabilities for strategic flexibility: A cognitive content framework. *European Journal of Marketing, 38*(11/12), 1456-1480.

Combe, I., Rajala, R., Westerlund, M., & Möller, K. (2012). Strategic flexibility in open innovation—Designing business models for open-source software. *European Journal of Marketing, 46*(10), 1368-1388.

Das, T. K. (1995). Managing strategic flexibility: Key to effective performance. *Journal of General Management, 20*(3), 60-75.

Drucker, P. F. (2010). *Toward the next economics: And other essays*. New York, NY: Harper & Row.

Ehrhart, M. G., & Klein, K. J. (2001). Predicting followers' preferences for charismatic leadership: The influence of follower values and personality. *The Leadership Quarterly, 12*(2), 153-179.

Gardner, J. W. (1990). *On leadership*. New York, NY: Simon and Schuster.

Gerwin, D. (1993). Manufacturing flexibility: A strategic perspective. *Management Science, 39*(4), 395-410.

Ghorban, R., & Gholipour, K. (2018). Investigating the impact of strategic flexibility on organizational innovation. *International Review of Management and Marketing, 8*(3), 1.

Gross, R. (2019). The constrained and the unconstrained strategist: A view of the firm. *Management Review: An International Journal, 14*(1), 4.

Johnson, J. L., Lee, R. P. W., Saini, A., & Grohmann, B. (2003). Market-focused strategic flexibility: Conceptual advances and an integrative model. *Journal of the Academy of Marketing Science, 31*(1), 74-89.

Kappel, F. R. (1960). *Vitality in a business enterprise.* New York, NY: McGraw-Hill.

Kellerman, B. (2008). *Followership: How followers are creating change and changing leaders.* Boston, MA: Harvard Business School Press.

Kelley, R. E. (1992). *The power of followership: How to create leaders people want to follow, and followers who lead themselves.* New York, NY: Doubleday/Currency.

Kim, S. (2018). Domains and trends of entrepreneurship research. *Management review: An International Journal, 13*(1), 65-90.

Kortmann, S., Gelhard, C., Zimmermann, C., & Piller, F. T. (2014). Linking strategic flexibility and operational efficiency: The mediating role of ambidextrous operational capabilities. *Journal of Operations Management, 32*(7-8), 475-490.

Krishnan, V. R. (2003). Power and moral leadership: Role of self–other agreement. *Leadership & Organization Development Journal, 24*(6), 345-351.

Malakyan, P. G. (2014). Followership in leadership studies: A case of leader–follower trade approach. *Journal of Leadership Studies, 7*(4), 6-22.

Meindl, J. R. (1995). The romance of leadership as a follower-centric theory: A social constructionist approach. *The Leadership Quarterly, 6*(3), 329-341.

Mintzberg, H. (1989). *Mintzberg on management: Inside our strange world of organizations.* New York, NY: Simon and Schuster.

Nanus, B. (1989). *The leader's edge: The seven keys to leadership in a turbulent world.* Chicago, IL: Contemporary Books.

Oc, B., & Bashshur, M. R. (2013). Followership, leadership, and social influence. *The Leadership Quarterly, 24*(6), 919-934.

Porter, M. E. (1985). *Competitive advantage: Creating and sustaining superior performance.* New York, NY: Free Press.

Salerno, J. T. (2008). The entrepreneur: real and imagined. *The Quarterly Journal of Austrian Economics, 11*(3-4), 188-207.

Sanchez, R. (1995). Strategic flexibility in product competition. *Strategic Management Journal, 16*(S1), 135-159.

Schepers, J., Wetzels, M., & de Ruyter, K. (2005). Leadership styles in technology acceptance: Do followers practice what leaders preach? *Managing Service Quality: An International Journal, 15*(6), 496-508.

Shimizu, K., & Hitt, M. A. (2004). Strategic flexibility: Organizational preparedness to reverse ineffective strategic decisions. *Academy of Management Perspectives, 18*(4), 44-59.

Srivastava, S., Sultan, A., & Chashti, N. (2017). Influence of innovation competence on firm-level competitiveness: An exploratory study. *Asia Pacific Journal of Innovation and Entrepreneurship, 11*(1), 63-75.

Sushil, X. (2001). Demythifying flexibility. *Management Decision, 39*(10), 860-865.

Tseng, C., & Tseng, C. (2019). Corporate entrepreneurship as a strategic approach for internal innovation performance. *Asia Pacific Journal of Innovation and Entrepreneurship, 13*(1), 108-120.

Uhl-Bien, M., & Pillai, R. (Eds.). (2007). The romance of leadership and the social construction of followership. Follower-centered perspectives on leadership: A tribute to the memory of James R. Meindl (pp. 187-209). Greenwich, CT: Information Age.

Volberda, H. W. (1996). Toward the flexible form: How to remain vital in hypercompetitive environments. *Organization Science, 7*(4), 359-374.

Wadhwa, S., & Bhagwat, R. (1998). Judicious increase in flexibility and decision automation in semi-computerized flexible manufacturing (SCFM) systems. *Studies in Informatics and Control, 7*(4), 329-342.

Wadhwa, S., & Rao, K. S. (2002). Towards a proactive flexibility management view. *Global Journal of Flexible Systems Management, 3*(2), 1-11.

Yukl, G. A., & Becker, W. S. (2006). Effective empowerment in organizations. *Organization Management Journal, 3*(3), 210-231.

Zhou, K. Z., & Wu, F. (2010). Technological capability, strategic flexibility, and product innovation. *Strategic Management Journal, 31*(5), 547-561.

Chapter 3:
Followership and Entrepreneurial Leadership

This chapter theoretically investigates the unexplored nature of followership in relation to another unexplored area of leadership— entrepreneurial leadership. However, minute writings delved into follower styles and an overabundance of research on leader styles. This chapter recognizes the critical role of those who faithfully and earnestly support leadership in pursuing novel endeavors. Extracting from literature on entrepreneurial leadership and the salient followership models, this study ascertains a vivid bipartite of the entrepreneurial leadership and follower styles.

Followership styles need further integration into the leadership domain. This assertion has been echoed by explorers to this vineyard. Additionally, a strain of the Austrian School view of entrepreneurship in this chapter is due to the fundamental need to describe the actions of those who seek to take risks, deal in uncertainty, and seek opportunity under the auspice of the firm. Followership and entrepreneurial leadership models are interwoven, highlighting the nexus between the two and illuminating potentialities for further investigation and inquiry.

INTRODUCTION

Many of the great organizations of our day have employed numerous types of knowledge bases (i.e., technical, functional, and managerial) to effectively compete and create competitive advantages in market economies (Chandler, 2009). These great organizations were led by leaders during their time who were not only entrepreneurial but transformative and became catalysts in strategically initiating learning bases. Organizations such as RCA, Philco, AT&T, IBM, Apple, Google, and Sun Systems—to name a few—were fueled by the ingenuity of their leadership and the ingenuity of their followers.

At Corning, great pride and attention were placed on employees who supported innovation to the point that division leaders rewarded followers who were committed to pioneering work. Smaller divisional entrepreneurial leadership allowed followers to pursue problem-solving projects that fueled their interests; there was a climate for those who did not want to be in the spotlight (Graham & Shuldiner, 2001). What was the connection between those who followed and those who led these organizations? Despite the robust amount of literature on leadership, there is much less in the vineyard of followership styles. Even Henry Ford described his most entrepreneurial subordinates as *tinkerers*, and the tinkerers were the subordinates (i.e., followers) who helped create the famous Model T (Zunz, 1992).

At the micro-level of the firm, there have been successful start-ups that had effective leadership, particularly Zenith and Raytheon, at the beginning of the electronics age boom (Chandler, 2009). Most, if not all, of these significant start-ups, were created by entrepreneurs and their followers. DHL (aka Daisey, Hillblom, & Lynn), the logistics company, was described as "something different" (Chung & Bowie, 2017, p. 26) as each carrier was "an integral part of the service chain" (p. 26). Nevertheless, DHL followers knew they were providing a means to an end for businesses across the world that was like no other provider at that time.

Quinn (1979) suggested that entrepreneurship is the most successful function in a market economy for meeting humans' newest needs. IBM, a company that meets business and consumer needs, is an excellent example of interfirm entrepreneurial leadership; they required their entrepreneurial leadership to possess high expertise, committed champions, and risk-taking support (Quinn, 1979). That is, IBM management "assembled first-rate people and supply [sic] them with a leader possessing extensive knowledge about their underlying art" (Quinn, 1979, p. 555). These examples show the dynamic relationship between leadership and followership, which transmits to the performance of the firm. Not all firms have a culture that allows for unhampered entrepreneurship—pervasive is management that leads through a change of environment but does not unhamper the entrepreneurial spirit when the time arises (Deal & Kennedy, 1982). Entrepreneurship has been discussed as an interorganizational role (Mintzberg, 1989) and as an initiator of planned change and controlled exploitation of opportunities (Yukl, 2009). Mintzberg (1989) described managers as decision-makers with one role— being entrepreneurial. Mintzberg wrote that the entrepreneurially minded manager leads projects and hands them down to subordinates when there is a project–job fit. Throughout the entrepreneurial literature, entrepreneurs have been described as decision-makers (Marshall, 1961; Mintzberg, 1989) and innovators who are disruptive to the climate (Schumpeter, 1934, 1963).

Entrepreneurs are purposeful, possess keen alertness to opportunity (Kirzner, 1997), and engage in activities in the marketplace (Mises, 1951). The conceptualization of human action was established by Mises (1949/1998), who suggested that the entrepreneur type displays leadership and purposeful human action with the strong characteristics of a promotor. There are gaps in the management, strategy, and leadership literature on the entrepreneurial qualities of leadership; however, value has been added and created by organizations who have historically possessed the followers and leaders who took the torch of exhibiting entrepreneurial characteristics to drive performance and profits and decrease losses (Foss & Klein, 2008).

One of the main issues with the follower–leader literature is the absence of clear examples that can inform how this dynamic relationship, as seen from followers, works at the firm level and its impact on the effectiveness of entrepreneurial leadership. That is the primary objective. Subsequently, a couple of questions arise: What is the nexus between followership styles and entrepreneurial leadership? Is there a one-to-one match between followers and certain entrepreneurial leaders?

Either way, the relationship is viewed in this chapter and starts a critical inquiry. Are certain follower styles more inclined to support leadership that is entrepreneurial? Is the relationship between followership style and entrepreneurial leadership temporal in nature? Over time, do followership styles change due to environmental changes, knowledge-based changes, or changes in the internal climate? These questions are analyzed using the management, leadership, and entrepreneurial leadership literature.

Another objective of this study is to integrate followership theory with entrepreneurial leadership theory that will, in effect, show that entrepreneurial leadership has to take into account the effectiveness of followership and to acknowledge that followers are active participants who play vital roles in creating and developing entrepreneurial pursuits (Crossman & Crossman, 2011). Küpers (2007) agreed that "followership has been an understudied topic in the academic literature; only little attention has been given to followers *sui generis*, who accord or withdraw support to leaders" (p. 195).

The lack of followership analysis and the typical notion that followers know how to follow and are mindless participants explain why the literature has not been fruitful. According to Crossman and Crossman (2011), leadership and followership have four major overlapping themes: (a) individualized or leader-centered theories, (b) leader-centered theories that rely on follower perspectives, (c) multiple leadership (shared/distributive), and (d) the follower *per se*. The current inquiry follows the latter category, *mutatis mutants*,

50

without a fully integrated connection with a specific type of leadership (i.e., entrepreneurial leadership).

Followership has been one of the least analyzed concepts (Crossman & Crossman, 2011) in the leadership, management, and entrepreneurship literature (Vecchio, 2003) but is one of the most active and participative roles in the leader–follower dyad (Kelley, 1992). Bjugstad, Thach, Thompson, and Morris (2006) reinforced this notion: "Followers and leaders are linked together in interrelated roles and are dependent on each other . . . [and] followership is what enables that leadership the opportunity to succeed" (p. 315).

While this is certainly true based on leadership principles and is broad in scope, it needs to be further examined from a followership perspective as to which type of follower is likely to be led by entrepreneurial leaders. Vecchio's (2003) statement leads this inquiry: "Followers who work for an entrepreneur/founder are likely to have more opportunities for greater interpersonal contact with the leader/founder, it is also worth considering what this increased contact may mean to each follower" (p. 316).

This inquiry is timely. It is intended to update the literature with a paradigm shift toward a more entrepreneurial organization and the climate of the current business landscape, which calls on subordinates and management to harness and exemplify entrepreneurial leadership institutionally between business units and teams. "The recognition and exploitation of new business opportunities are called for in entrepreneurship research" (Hoskisson, Covin, Volberda, & Johnson, 2011, p. 144). This chapter consists of a literature review, implications, and conclusion.

LITERATURE REVIEW

Followership Styles and Models

Kelley (1988, 1992) is one of the most prominent proponents of followership; Kelley set the stage with a model that is very much the basis for the current inquiry in this topic domain. Because followership has been an understudied and observed phenomenon, there has been a mixed review of the importance and role of followers. Kelley (2008) described the basic view of the conceptualization of followership: "These folks believed that being a strong #2 often allowed for greater contributions than being in the #1 spot and that making the assist was just as important as making the score. Many had no desire to be leaders" (p. 6).

Followership has been, in its broadest sense, described as participants in a team effort, active participants who act with enthusiasm and independence, and both think critically and act (Kelley, 1992). Kelley (1992) provided one of the most salient models in the followership literature. According to Kelley's model, there are five followership styles: alienated, exemplary, passive, conformist, and pragmatist. The axis of each followership style is broken down into four categorical quadrants: independent thinkers, critical thinkers, dependent, uncritical thinkers, and passive or active thinkers.

Kelly (1992) contended that alienated followers embody a healthy skepticism about the organization. They think critically, do not participate in group or team environments, and are highly independent. Exemplary followers are independent thinkers and actively engaged when it comes to working with others. Passive followers rely heavily on leadership to do all of their thinking and need excessive direction and orders; this type of followership is characterized by low participation and low independent thinking. Conformist followers are willing to take orders and are likely to wait on leadership to point the direction. This follower type is very active but is low on independent thinking. Kelley called this type of follower *yes* people. Lastly, pragmatist followers are in the *middle* when it comes to the characterizations of the other four follower styles (Kellerman, 2008; Kelley, 1992).

Chaleff (1997) developed a model that closely relates to that developed by Kelley (1992). With a few differences in the description of the four follower types, the general idea postulates followers' power and subsequent development (Kellerman, 2008). Chaleff's model has four followership styles based on the degree of follower support to leadership (i.e., high or low) and how followers challenge leadership (i.e., high or low): implementer, partner, individualist, and resource.

Chaleff (1997) asserted that the implementer is the most common style because superiors depend on this type to get things done, especially in larger organizations. The partner supports leadership initiatives but is willing to challenge leadership if the situation calls for it. Individualists are open about their feelings and ideas, challenge leadership, and at times withhold their support. Individuals with a resource follower style work honestly *for a few day's pay* but will not go beyond what is expected of them. The four followership styles are separated into four quadrants: high support, low support, high challenge, and low challenge. The implementer is high support and low challenge, the partner style is high support and high challenge, the individualist style is high challenge and low support, and the resource style is low challenge low support.

Baker (2007) developed followership criteria and outlined that (a) followership pertains to a role, (b) followership is active and not passive, (c) followership and leadership share a common purpose, and (d) the relationship between followers and leaders is significant. Are all followers the same? Bjugstad et al. (2006) suggested there are effective and ineffective followers and that a distinction should be made to understand the impact of followership on organizational performance. Agho (2009) and Bjugstad et al. both characterized the follower in a light that presupposes the follower to be just as engaged in performance and impact as the given leader. Given the hierarchal nature of many organizations, followers are honest, creditable, and self-initiated in process and goals that are aligned with the organizational leadership (Agho, 2009; Bjugstad et al., 2006). Agho asserted, "Failure to recognize followership as a complement of leadership may undermine organizational effectiveness and efficiency" (p. 2).

Agho's (2009) line of analysis of the follower was initiated from a study where 302 senior-level executives were probed about their perception of effective followers (and leaders). Agho found distinct, yet significant, differences between effective followers and leaders. Bjugstad et al. (2006) asserted that effective followers are enthusiastic, self-reliant, and positively participate in organizational goals. Like Bjugstad et al., Agho characterized followers with similar but different adjectives: mature, caring, dependable, inspiring, and forward-looking. Using a follower-centered approach, Uhl-Bien, Riggio, Lowe, and Carsten (2014) asserted, "The fundamental attribution error leads followers to over-attribute causality for group outcomes to the leader" (p. 86).

Entrepreneurial Leadership

McGrath and MacMillian (2000) clearly explained the role and function of entrepreneurial leadership. First, entrepreneurial leaders find novel ways to harness opportunities and find competitive insights within the firm; second, entrepreneurial leaders seek novel and practical activities to employ and encourage others to discard ineffective activities (McGrath & MacMillian, 2000). Entrepreneurial initiatives are sought by this type of leadership because entrepreneurial leaders are path definers and push to clear paths to develop a learning base for new opportunity exploitation.

From an entrepreneurial leadership perspective, three activities fall under entrepreneurial leadership: set the climate, orchestrate the process of realizing opportunity, and solve problems with others on new ventures to grow the business (McGrath & MacMillian, 2000). Kuratko (2007) most effectively described entrepreneurial leadership as "a dynamic process of vision, change, and creation. It requires an application of energy and passion towards the creation and implementation of new ideas and creative solutions" (p. 3). The entrepreneurial type of leadership has roots in the traditional forms of leadership that are so often articulated in the leadership literature; however, entrepreneurial leadership is one of the most neglected areas of leadership and needs to be integrated into the research agenda (Antonakis & Autio, 2007; Vecchio, 2003).

One of the main areas of departure between leadership and entrepreneurial leadership is that entrepreneurial leader's influence and motivate others to pursue entrepreneurial goals (Gupta, MacMillan, & Surie, 2004). This departure is significant due to the closeness of entrepreneurial leaders with the often-debated characteristics of entrepreneurs. Moravec (1994) reinforced the notion of diversion between entrepreneurial leadership and other leadership by noting that "corporations now undergo paradigm shifts rather than linear change. One such paradigm shift is from a 'producer mentality' that seeks instructions to an 'entrepreneurial mentality'" (p. 4) that seeks results. Greenberger and Sexton (1988), for example, said, "entrepreneurs are likely to have some abstract image in mind about what they intend to accomplish . . . [and they] must be able to create a similar image in the minds of others" (p. 5).

Surie and Ashley (2007) echoed other definitions of entrepreneurial leadership that find it to be a function where "leadership [is] capable of sustaining innovation and adaptation in high-velocity and uncertain environments" (p. 235). Kuratko (2007) established that entrepreneurial leaders are risk-takers, idea champions, prime innovators, and unintentionally cross-sectional in efforts to establish direction for the firm.

Importantly, entrepreneurial leaders are willing to change direction. They have a high tolerance for ambiguous situations and uncertain futures (Guth & Ginsberg, 1990; Sathe, 1985). The firm employs entrepreneurial leadership as a proponent to secure competitive advantages in market economies by being path definers and first movers—transferring individual capabilities to organizational capabilities (Chandler, 2009). Building and creating competitive advantages entail a path-defining learning orientation and transferring capabilities, which Fernald, Solomon, and Tarabishy (2005) forthrightly provided. Entrepreneurial leaders create and drive a vision for the future, solve problems, take risks, and initiate strategies—placing structures in a position to flex entrepreneurship within the firm (Fernald et al., 2005). Entrepreneurial leaders are problem solvers who clear paths and define learning paths that would otherwise go unnoticed. This type of leadership expands absorptive capacity and communicates and transmits values to action in entrepreneurial goals. Therefore, the undistinguishable role of entrepreneurial leaders is to shoulder the burden of *risks* and *uncertainty*, unlike any other form of leadership

(Knight, 1921). In Gartner's (1988) words, the "entrepreneur . . . [causes] entrepreneurship" (p. 48).

With the primary objective in mind—connecting followership style with entrepreneurial leadership—the theoretical framework explores the different followership styles against the characteristics of entrepreneurial leadership. These two theories have not been integrated or established to understand whether it matters if there is a connection between exemplary followership and entrepreneurial leadership. There may not be a match of each characteristic, but the characteristics should be viewed as a spectrum because other factors should be considered, such as organizational climate, psychological factors, preferences, etc. Figures 1 and 2 display two models of followership (Kelley, 1992, Chaleff, 1997) that contrast entrepreneurial leadership characteristics.

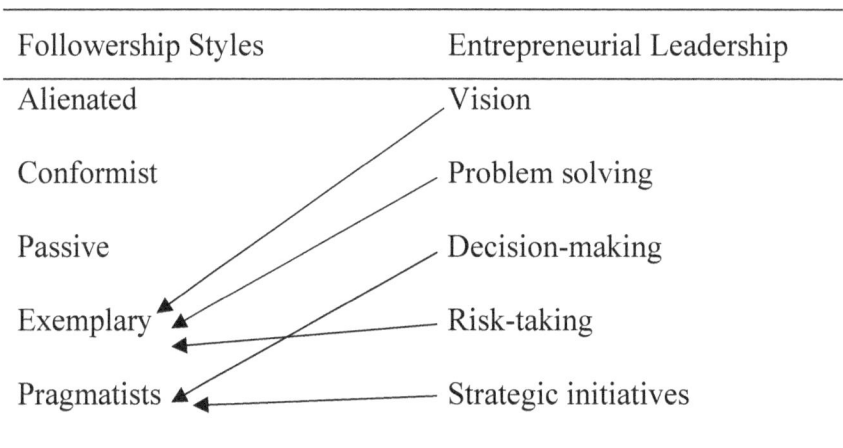

Followership Styles	Entrepreneurial Leadership
Alienated	Vision
Conformist	Problem solving
Passive	Decision-making
Exemplary	Risk-taking
Pragmatists	Strategic initiatives

Figure 1. Kelley's (1992) followership styles contrasted with entrepreneurial leadership.

Followership Styles	Entrepreneurial Leadership
The implementer	Risk-taker
The partner	Idea champion
The individualist	Prime innovator
The resource follower	Tolerance for ambiguity
	Cross-sectional work relations

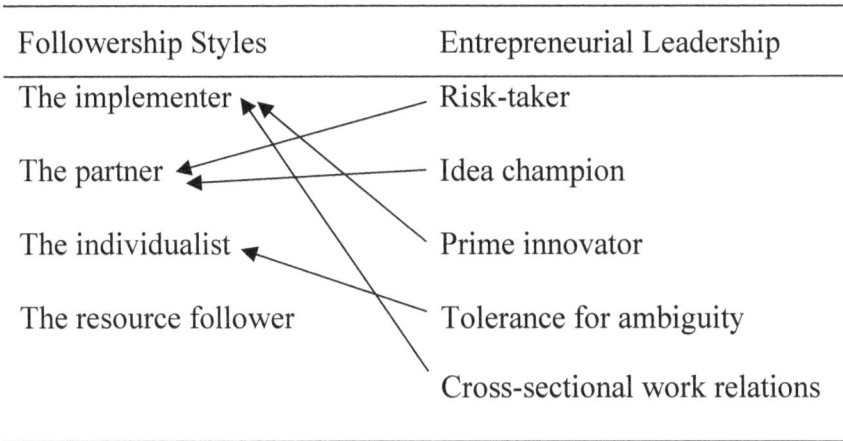

*Figure 2. Chaleff's (1997) followership styles contrasted with
entrepreneurial leadership.*

The figures show the connections among nine followership styles and 10 characteristics of entrepreneurial leaders. Based on these two models, not all followership styles coincide with entrepreneurial leadership.

Some follower styles do not align with the nature of what is characterized by entrepreneurial leadership. Some follower styles might pose a hindrance to those who are entrepreneurial (i.e., those pursuing entrepreneurial goals within the organizational context). There seems to be more evenly connected entrepreneurial leadership characterizations between Chaleff's (1997) followership styles and Kuratko's (2007) entrepreneurial leadership. These assertions follow that followers' styles are driven "internally, and a leader merely taps into the internal power of the follower" (Bjugstad et al., 2006, p. 306). The figures also show relationships that might reflect a causal relationship "between follower and leader and how well their characteristics match up" (Bjugstad et al., 2006, p. 306).

Tables 1 and 2 depict a more focused linkage between followership styles and one that is more likely to be led by or with entrepreneurial leaders with characteristics specified by Fernald et al. (2005) and Kuratko (2007). While the information in these tables is not intended to provide a perfect match, it initiates a theoretical perspective that needs further qualitative or quantitative analysis and testing. With that in mind, casual observation of Table 1 might illustrate some primary followership motivations, which is even more illuminated in Table 2. Chaleff's (1997) followership styles seem to be based on firm-level orientation. This is a rather significant point because Chaleff's followership styles are primarily concerned with followership development rather than leadership and its effect on followers (Kellerman, 2008).

Table 1
Followership Styles (Kelley, 1992) and Entrepreneurial Leadership (Fernald et al., 2005)

Followership Styles	Entrepreneurial Leadership Characteristics
Exemplary	Vision
	Problem-solving
	Risk-taking
Pragmatist	Decision-making
	Strategic initiatives

Table 2
Followership Styles (Chaleff, 1997) and Entrepreneurial Leadership (Kuratko, 2007)

Followership Styles	Entrepreneurial Leadership Characteristics
Partner	Risk-taker
	Idea champion
Individualist	Prime innovator
	Tolerance for ambiguity
Implementer	Cross-sectional work relations

IMPLICATIONS

First-mover firms have an advantage over path-follower firms in a market exchange economy. In order to define paths and develop a firm's strength embedded in a learning base, it is insightful to understand the follower–entrepreneurial leadership connection. There is a litany of perspectives and propositions on the traits, characteristics, and consequences of leadership, but there is an urgent need to understand the followership styles primed to be led by entrepreneurial leaders. Knowing what this synthesis between followership styles and entrepreneurial leadership looks like in the firm is equally advantageous.

An absence of leadership, no doubt, interrupts the transmission of values and vision needed to form an entrepreneurial spirit (Soriano & Martinez, 2007). To take it another step, it is a dynamic between followers and their style and a generic entrepreneurial spirit that leads the charge. The specificity of designation between follower and leader can be nullified—as this dynamic is circumventable. The reality of this dynamic is that all too often there are mismatches where leaders are unfamiliar with or do not perceive the motivations or the style of subordinates' followership at any point in time. Many extraneous variables could perhaps incentivize an adapted followership style and those that can disincentivize the same.

With today's firms ever more searching for competitive positioning and exploring innovative techniques to bolster effectiveness, entrepreneurial leadership has to be a proponent of and advocate for those people who take pride in a supporting role— those "without the most glamorous work and without the fanfare" (Wren, 1995, p. 196). Firms that can rely on effective followers benefit from the advantages profit from their self-assertiveness and commitment to the purpose of their work. While there are many reasons followers are vital to the performance of the firm, some of the most impactful reasons are that they are continuous learners of skills and education useful to the firm and frequently hold higher performance standards than is required in their work environment (Wren, 1995).

Entrepreneurial leadership is not only an inherent characteristic that individuals possess at any point in time but a phenomenon that is cultivated by the climate of the firm and the external environment. Constrained strategists are likely to hamper an entrepreneurial environment, while unconstrained strategists are more likely to unleash the entrepreneurial spirit, thus allowing for a connection between the follower style and entrepreneurial fit to take place. This implies that structure must consider the possibility for there to be a follower style fit and relations and motivations to merge in order to drive follower motivation to link with entrepreneurial leaders. Because there is no such thing as entrepreneurial leadership styles, it would be difficult to speak on a possible goal for entrepreneurial leadership *per se*. If entrepreneurial leadership was categorically placed into styles, it would then be feasible to place a goal orientation on a style; however, entrepreneurial leaders visualize and are motivated toward goals both intentionally and unintentionally. Due to the inherent inflexibility of models, the two followership models constrain the flesh-and-blood real-world situations where follower styles may change temporally or situationally as with leadership styles (Bjugstad et al., 2006; Uhl-Bien et al., 2014).

CONCLUSION

There is only a handful of literature on followership; only a few authors have been willing to explore this area. Therefore, this theoretical perspective established a few points worthy of mention. This chapter built on the most salient models in the followership area as developed by Kelley (1992) and Chaleff (1997) and developed the perspective that indeed there might be followership styles linked with a unique type of leadership, specifically entrepreneurial leadership. This chapter developed two models to show specific followership styles connected with the specified entrepreneurial characteristics provided by Kuratko (2007) and Fernald et al. (2005). Finally, this chapter introduced two integrative concepts into the leadership literature that will be advantageous for further exploration and empirical testing.

REFERENCES

Agho, A. O. (2009). Perspectives of senior-level executives on effective followership and leadership. *Journal of Leadership & Organizational Studies, 16*(2), 159-166.

Antonakis, J., & Autio, E. (2007). *Entrepreneurship and leadership: The psychology of entrepreneurship.* Mahwah, NJ: Lawrence Erlbaum Associates, Inc.

Baker, S. D. (2007). Followership: The theoretical foundation of a contemporary construct. *Journal of Leadership & Organizational Studies, 14*(1), 50-60.

Bjugstad, K., Thach, E. C., Thompson, K. J., & Morris, A. (2006). A fresh look at followership: A model for matching followership and leadership styles. *Journal of Behavioral and Applied Management, 7*(3), 304.

Chaleff, I. (1997). The courageous follower: Standing up to and for our leaders. *NASSP Bulletin, 81*(586), 119-119.

Chandler, A. D., Jr. (2009). *Inventing the electronic century: The epic story of the consumer electronics and computer industries.* Cambridge, MA: Harvard University Press.

Chung, P., & Bowie, R. (2017). *DHL: From startup to global upstart.* Berlin, Germany: Walter de Gruyter GmbH.

Crossman, B., & Crossman, J. (2011). Conceptualising followership—A review of the literature. *Leadership, 7*(4), 481-497.

Deal, T. E., & Kennedy, A. A. (1982). *Corporate cultures.* Reading, MA: Addison Wesley.

Fernald, L. W., Solomon, G. T., & Tarabishy, A. (2005). A new paradigm: Entrepreneurial leadership. *Southern Business Review, 30*(2), 1-10.

Foss, N. J., & Klein, P. G. (2008, January 29). *Entrepreneurship: From opportunity discovery to judgment* (SMG Working Paper No. 5). Retrieved from SSRN website: https://ssrn.com/abstract=1098144 or http://dx.doi.org/10.213 9/ssrn.1098144

Gartner, W. B. (1988). "Who is an entrepreneur?" is the wrong question. *American Journal of Small Business, 12*(4), 11-32.

Graham, M. B., & Shuldiner, A. T. (2001). *Corning and the craft of innovation.* New York, NY: Oxford University Press.

Greenberger, D. B., & Sexton, D. L. (1988). An interactive model of new venture initiation. *Journal of Small Business Management, 26*(3), 1-7.

Gupta, V., MacMillan, I. C., & Surie, G. (2004). Entrepreneurial leadership: Developing and measuring a cross-cultural construct. *Journal of Business Venturing, 19*(2), 241-260.

Guth, W. D., & Ginsberg, A. (1990). Guest editors' introduction: Corporate entrepreneurship. *Strategic Management Journal, 11*, 5-15.

Hoskisson, R. E., Covin, J., Volberda, H. W., & Johnson, R. A. (2011). Revitalizing entrepreneurship: The search for new research opportunities. *Journal of Management Studies, 48*(6), 1141-1168.

Kellerman, B. (2008). *Followership: How followers are creating change and changing leaders.* Boston, MA: Harvard Business School Press.

Kelley, R. E. (1988, November). In praise of followers. *Harvard Business Review.* Retrieved from https://hbr.org/1988/11/in-praise-of-followers

Kelley, R. E. (1992). *The power of followership: How to create leaders people want to follow, and followers who lead themselves.* New York, NY: Broadway Business.

Kelley, R. E. (2008). Rethinking followership. In R. E. Riggio, I. Chaleff, & J. Lipman-Blumen (Eds.), *The art of followership: How great followers create great leaders and organizations* (pp. 5-16). San Francisco, CA: Jossey-Bass.

Kirzner, I. M. (1997). Entrepreneurial discovery and the competitive market process: An Austrian approach. *Journal of Economic Literature, 35*(1), 60-85.

Knight, F. (1921). *Risk, uncertainty and profit.* New York, NY: Augustus Kelley.

Küpers, W. (2007). Perspectives on integrating leadership and followership. *International Journal of Leadership Studies*, *2*(3), 194-221.

Kuratko, D. F. (2007). Entrepreneurial leadership in the 21st century: Guest editor's perspective. *Journal of Leadership & Organizational Studies*, *13*(4), 1-11.

Marshall, A. (1961). *Principles of economics*. London, England: Macmillan for the Royal Economic Society.

McGrath, R. G., & MacMillan, I. C. (2000). *The entrepreneurial mindset: Strategies for continuously creating opportunity in an age of uncertainty* (Vol. 284). Boston, MA: Harvard Business Press.

Mintzberg, H. (1989). *Mintzberg on management: Inside our strange world of organizations*. New York, NY: Simon and Schuster.

Mises, L. V. (1951). Profit and loss. *Planning for Freedom*, 108-150.

Mises, L. V. (1998). *Human action: A treatise on economics*. Auburn, AL: Ludwig von Mises Institute. (Original work published 1949)

Moravec, M. (1994). Leaders must love change, not loathe it. *HR Focus*, *71*(2), 13-13.

Quinn, J. B. (1979). Technological innovation, entrepreneurship, and strategy. *Sloan Management Review (pre-1986)*, *20*(3), 19-30.

Sathe, V. (1985). How to decipher and change corporate culture. In R. H. Kilmann, M. J. Saxton, R. Serpa, & Associates, *Gaining control of the corporate culture* (pp. 230-261). San Francisco, CA: Jossey-Bass.

Schumpeter, J. A. (1934). *The theory of economic development*. Cambridge, MA: Harvard University Press.

Schumpeter, J. A. (1963). *History of economic analysis*. New York, NY: Oxford University Press.

Soriano, R. D., & Martínez, J. M. C. (2007). Transmitting the entrepreneurial spirit to the work team in SMEs: The

importance of leadership. *Management Decision, 45*(7),
1102-1122.

Surie, G., & Ashley, A. (2007). Integrating pragmatism and ethics
in entrepreneurial leadership for sustainable value creation.
Journal of Business Ethics, 81(1), 235-246.

Uhl-Bien, M., Riggio, R. E., Lowe, K. B., & Carsten, M. K.
(2014). Followership theory: A review and research agenda.
The Leadership Quarterly, 25(1), 83-104.

Vecchio, R. P. (2003). Entrepreneurship and leadership: Common
trends and common threads. *Human Resource Management
Review, 13*(2), 303-327.

Wren, J. T. (1995). *The leader's companion: Insights on
leadership through the ages.* New York, NY: Simon and
Schuster.

Yukl, G. (2009). Leading organizational learning: Reflections on
theory and research. *The Leadership Quarterly, 20*(1), 49-53.

Zunz, O. (1992). *Making America Corporate, 1870-1920.* Chicago,
IL: University of Chicago Press.

Chapter 4:
Entrepreneurial Leadership and Organizational Flexibility

This chapter provides numerous contributions to the entrepreneurial leadership and organizational flexibility literature. This is due to two main crosscurrents in the business landscape: the plasticity of the entrepreneurial leader as a creator of a firm's competitive advantages and the ever-changing, agile firm that competes in extremely unstable marketplace environments.

The dimensions of organizational flexibility (i.e., competitiveness, operational, and strategic flexibility) are configured into a new theoretical framework. This theoretical examination derived five future research questions hypothesized to be attributed to the transitional dynamics of flexibility. The barriers to organizational flexibility and the effects of entrepreneurial leadership are theoretically examined using existing literature in these areas.

Inherent in all human endeavors, this study is not without its limitations. Unique theoretical postulates and research questions are developed for future researchers to explore in this mosaic vineyard. Future research should approach these areas from the firm level and individual level of analysis to establish a full conception of the interplay between the individual and the firm. This theoretical framework is unique and has not been addressed or written about in extant management, strategic leadership, and organizational literature. Entrepreneurial leadership is explored historically and in its contemporary sui generis nature within the firm.

INTRODUCTION

Entrepreneurship and leadership are not synonymous, nor are they antithetical in producing results; but when fused, they form a driving force called *entrepreneurial leadership* (Renko, El Tarabishy, Carsrud, & Brännback, 2015). Leadership in and of itself is an influential and transformative mechanism between people and processes within the enterprise (Yukl, 2009). When entrepreneurship and leadership flourish within the firm, it creates an internal climate of collaboration and effective use of ingenuity that sets off a trajectory of opportunity-seeking goals (Child, 2015; Mintzberg & Waters, 1985; Newman, Herman, Schwarz, & Nielsen, 2018).

On the other end of the spectrum, organizational rigidity is the result of preservation and is rooted in the stability paradigm (Mintzberg, 1990). There has been a shift away from organizational rigidity due to a greater awareness of the benefits of organizational plasticity, changeability, and agility (Roberts & Stockport, 2009; Sharma & Jain, 2010; Volberda, 1998). At this theoretical crosscurrent between rigidity and flexibility, there must be an examination from an entrepreneurial leadership perspective to identify the attributes, values, and characteristics of entrepreneurial leadership and the organizational behaviors that can overcome the barriers to organizational flexibility. Even Kanter (1983) categorized organizational barriers as bureaucratic traps and entrepreneurial traps. The entrepreneurial trap leads to a single-minded push of ideas as the individual must be the source of new ideas (Kanter, 1983). Thus, flexibility has been viewed as a social condition and not a phenomenon as an individual consequence.

Entrepreneurial leadership is a set of attitudes and behaviors that can be set in motion but can also be constrained by structure, communication, and policy. The entrepreneur has been described as a dynamic function within a marketplace and within the firm. The entrepreneurial leader is the one who assumes the risks of uncertainty (Knight, 1933), and the decision-maker discovers new market opportunities (Kirzner, 1973) or one who supplies the financial capital (Mises, 1949) that leads to action in the marketplace.

The entrepreneur—as an individual—acts as an innovator (Schumpeter, 1934), discoverer (Kirzner, 1997), and the corporate initiator of new processes (Kuratko, Hornsby, & Goldsby, 2007). It is the entrepreneur's role to strategize flexible mechanisms when change and market adaptation is warranted (Volberda, 1998). That is keeping in mind that organizational flexibility is at the nexus of individual behaviors and competencies and organizational resources (Volberda, 1998). While taking a few of the entrepreneurial descriptors into account, innovation and risk-seeking behaviors must involve other non-entrepreneurs and management buy-in in the uphill battle of maximizing the firm's entrepreneurial spirit. It has been noted that for some firms, inefficiency is the norm (Leibenstein, 1968). When leadership pursues an entrepreneurial trajectory, it evokes internal change, then organizational barriers ensue, followed by employee resistance. This study pertains to entrepreneurial behaviors of leadership as the primary catalyst for the dissolution of organizational barriers and resistance to flexibility.

Entrepreneurship is the dark corner of the business and economics literature (Hébert & Link, 1982), but it represents creative, innovative, and purposeful action and keen alertness for opportunity (Kirzner 1997; Mises, 1949). Leadership, when added to entrepreneurial behaviors, provides strategic vision (Mintzberg, 1989), a fusion of purpose (Bass & Avolio, 1994), and a culture of collaboration, inspiration, and energy (Northouse, 2007). How does entrepreneurial leadership coincide with a firm's flexibility? How can incumbent firms compete with newcomers without being flexible? Questions of great importance but rarely discussed are: How can incumbent firms become more flexible? How can they work through emerging and serendipitous strategies?

These inquiries are not only in line with the already *sui generis* nature of the entrepreneur but also make a closer examination as to how entrepreneurial leadership impacts flexibility within a given firm because entrepreneurs create the entrepreneurial spirit that links leaders and followers (Gross, 2019). To date, only a small amount of research has delved into the nature of entrepreneurial leadership within the firm, but these studies have generally shied away from any tangible determinates. There is a need for further theoretical connection with firm-level determinates and some interfirm context in understanding the nature of entrepreneurial leadership, particularly firm-level flexibility (Renko et al., 2015).

This chapter is similar in substance to the salient work of Mintzberg and Westley's (1992) cycles of change, whereby landscape dynamics create cycles of change that act more like a *system of moving circles*, as change happens either deductively or inductively. Entrepreneurial leadership is an inductive force. Entrepreneurial leadership is likely to have some level of impact on a firm's flexibility, notwithstanding the many enterprise barriers that slow down the momentum of the entrepreneurial spirit (Leibenstein, 1968). As the saying goes, "a change in thinking with no change in action" (Mintzberg & Westley, 1992, p. 41) cannot positively contribute to firm flexibility. A firm's flexibility derives from the force of change, and because change is constant, all firms are subject to it. For example, employees' names change, operations change, and customers change. Hence, "a company must be flexible" (Rodgers, 1992, p. 18).

In this regard, several theorists have shown how important and relevant entrepreneurial leadership is when starting corporate ventures, innovating, and implementing internal strategic initiatives (Barbuto, 2016; Fernald, Solomon, & Tarabishy, 2005; Hmieleski & Ensley, 2007; Mintzberg & Waters, 1985; Renko et al., 2015). Organizational flexibility is the potentiality of a given firm's response, at any time or market, to competitive market pressures and market signals due to the degree of competitiveness in the business landscape (Brozovic, 2018). Environmental factors that impact flexibility include regulations, technologies, competitors, and even strategic model reengineering—factors that point to the probability of changing internal circumstances. Because firms sell products and offer services in consumer markets, there tends to be a relevant concern as to the extent to which the firm can increase flexibility in order to meet market demands and compete in hotly contested consumer markets. There is an attempt to convey the relevancy of entrepreneurial leadership in an organization's pursuit of organizational flexibility. The importance of entrepreneurial leadership as a transitioning force and facilitator of flexibility is a focal point because flexibility is a firm's ability to adapt to market changes and environments (Atkinson, 1985; Kouropalatis, Hughes, & Morgan, 2012; Scott & Meyer, 1994).

The current study follows similar views held by other authors (Brozovic, 2018; Fernald et al., 2005; Leitch & Volery, 2017; Mintzberg & Waters, 1985; Mintzberg & Westley, 1992; Renko et al., 2015; Shane & Venkataraman, 2000) in that entrepreneurial leadership primarily involves processes, people, structure, and strategy-making and seeking to exploit future-oriented opportunity (Fernald et al., 2005; Kirzner, 1999). Flexible organizations are able to deal with changes in the environment or internal management systems (Carlsson, 1999; Chowdary, 2001; De Groote, 1994). Additionally, organizational flexibility involves freedom of choice and the creation of options within the firm. Entrepreneurial leadership is best explained as a force of influence—a dynamic process that embodies vision, change, and creation (Kuratko et al., 2007; Sushil, 2000). Kuratko et al. (2007) contended that entrepreneurial leadership "requires an application of energy and passion towards the creation and implementation of new ideas and creative solutions" (p. 3). Therefore, the use of entrepreneurial leadership employed to dismantle the barriers to a more flexible organization effectively has yet to be explored—quantitatively, qualitatively, or theoretically.

This inquiry is significant because current entrepreneurial leadership literature does not reveal the importance of this type of leadership in adapting serendipitous approaches to interfirm decision-making and strategy-making through the lens of entrepreneurial action. Additionally, this chapter explores the transitional force behind a firm's adaptation to market changes and competitive pressures that facilitate the ability to capture positive unintended consequences through entrepreneurial leadership

(Coulson-Thomas, 2015). According to Antonakis and Autio (2007), entrepreneurial leadership is a "neglected area of entrepreneurial research" (p. 189), and "entrepreneurship could stand to gain from a closer integration with leadership research" (p. 203). Albeit on theoretical grounds, there is a need to examine the literature for possible connections between entrepreneurial leadership and organizational flexibility.

Internal barriers to organizational flexibility are examined with an inside-out perspective. The following question guides this examination: How can entrepreneurial leadership impact organizational flexibility barriers? This inquiry is timely because contemporary firms face increasing competition and more consumer demands, relying more on value-added activities than ever before (Sharma & Jain, 2010). In today's market economy, firms must have flexible capability to change and uncertainty or the competitive advantage to avoid change. Quick, rapid, but well-structured responses to market signals are not the exception but the rule, which impacts a firm's resources positively and negatively (Parnell, 2005).

The answer to why this line of inquiry persists can be attributed to Leitch and Volery (2017), who proposed that more studies are needed to examine the nature of interorganizational entrepreneurial leadership. There is no question that management and leadership must initiate flexible changes and adjust, lead with vision, solve problems, take risks, and initiate strategy (Fernald et al., 2005). If the firm remains flexible, then management assumes an open-system approach; however, at some level, there is inherent interorganizational resistance to change (Gromoff, Kazantsev, Kozhevnikov, Ponfilenok, & Stavenko, 2012). Change and flexibility are interwoven catalysts, which open an inquiry into whether entrepreneurial leadership must be a conveyor of the vision and influence needed to pursue a trajectory of organizational flexibility. The remainder of this chapter reviews entrepreneurial leadership and organizational flexibility and proposes a theoretical framework. The chapter concludes with future research considerations.

LITERATURE REVIEW

Entrepreneurial Leadership

Much has been written and hypothesized about the individual entrepreneur and corporate venturing; however, few have clearly added to the theoretical nature of entrepreneurial leadership as an active participant within the firm. Is entrepreneurial leadership axiomatically associated with the rugged bootstrapping of a small upstart, or is there a need to further explicate what is meant by entrepreneurial leadership that operates within a firm and perhaps under the auspice of management? Because there is a narrow distinction between management and entrepreneurial behaviors, it is profitable to discern a few definitions of entrepreneurial leadership.

As such, Surie and Ashley (2008) defined entrepreneurial leadership as a firm that is "capable of sustaining innovation and adaptation in high-velocity and uncertain environments" (p. 235). Roomi and Harrison (2011) added that entrepreneurial leadership works as "a fusion of these two constructs: having and communicating the vision to engage teams to identify, develop, and take advantage of opportunity in order to gain competitive advantage" (p. 1). Kuratko et al. (2007) said that entrepreneurial leadership is "a dynamic process of vision, change, and creation. It requires an application of energy and passion towards the creation and implementation of new ideas and creative solutions" (p. 3). What has not been added to the rather broad definitions of entrepreneurial leadership is that entrepreneurial leadership is a competitive tool, imitable to any given firm at any given time and marketplace and is a creator of competitive advantage by using vision and influence during times of uncertainty and risk-taking.

The very idea that leadership has a function in a marketplace has been proclaimed by many theorists in the economics area (Hébert & Link, 1982); however, only a few prominent economists have delved into the role of the entrepreneur as a leader in a marketplace. For example, a prominent Austrian economist said that an entrepreneur is one who displays purposeful human action and has the characteristics of leadership. Over the centuries, many schools of economic thought out of the Austrian School, the Harvard Tradition, the German Historical School, and the Neoclassical School have provided increments of discourse concerning the nature of entrepreneurship. Of course, the conceptualization of market action was insightfully established by Ludwick von Mises out of the Austrian School. However, Mises was not the only voice in this long line of discussion related to the vital quest to define the *ideal* entrepreneur and what they do and how this is at variance with non-entrepreneurs. A few have voiced that entrepreneurship is taking on inherent risk (Knight, 1933), that is, the entrepreneur is a disruptive innovator (Schumpeter, 1934). Additionally, Salerno (2008) distinguished between those who can act on leadership principles entrepreneurially and those who cannot be entrepreneurial due to their inability to adjust and move swiftly to changing conditions in the marketplace. Salerno said that it is "the quality of leadership possessed by those who introduce new products or radically new methods of producing old products" (p. 194).

In this sense, the entrepreneur assumes capital risks to create combinations that are intended to change conditions not only for one's own sake but for the satisfaction and desires of customers (Rothbard, 1985, p. 547). Schumpeter (1950) said that the entrepreneur is anyone within a firm who pursues new combinations of resources. These combinations include the combination of firms and/or the mobility of resources toward new allocations. Entrepreneurs seek ways to act in the market that reflect their purpose, skills, creativity, and ability to recombine resources based on external opportunities.

Entrepreneurial leadership provides internal capability, knowledge, and distinctive competency and transmits the climate of vision and values needed to energize the innovative behaviors conducive to increasing the firm's competitive advantage. Entrepreneurial leadership is not only for start-ups but is also necessary for incumbent firms to compete with newcomer firms to fight for market-dominant designs. Entrepreneurial leadership serves the life of the firm past the start-up phase of business operations.

Organizational Flexibility

Sushil (2001) and Roberts and Stockport (2009) agreed that flexibility of the enterprise has been well documented and conceived in several writings (Handy, 1995; Kanter, 1994; Peters, 1987; Steers, 1975). However, it was Volberda (1999) who provided four categories of firms: (a) rigid, (b) planned, (c) flexible, and (d) chaotic. Relating to flexible organizations, three approaches were provided: (a) general, (b) functional, and (c) actor (Sharma, & Jain, 2010; Sushil, 2001; Volberda, 1999). The actor approach to flexibility specifically focuses on the values and behaviors within the firm (Volberda, 1999). The actor's behaviors are either self-constrained or unconstrained as firms approach a transition in their paradigm of flexibility. The actor approach "highlights the important roles and traits of different functions in developing flexibility, such as the character of the *entrepreneur* (uncertainty creating or reducing), *management* (risk rewarding or risk-averse) employees (satisfaction by routines or variety)" (Volberda, 1999, p. 4). That is, unconstrained characteristics tend to be more conducive to organizational flexibility.

In a general sense, organizational flexibility (Sushil, 2001) can be described by the following dimensions: adaptiveness, openness, responsiveness, change, freedom, agility, reliance, and customization. van der Weerdt, Volberda, Verwaal, and Stienstra (2012) stated, "Flexibility is perceived to be a managerial task" (p. 15). This assertion points to the capabilities of management and leadership in flexible firms. It can be assumed that the leadership of flexible organizations is tasked with challenging uncertainty, affecting change, and maintaining continuity: these are important issues facing managers. However, little is known about the determinates of entrepreneurial leadership facilitation of organizational flexibility. Flexibility and leadership have interactive effects on firm-level performance, mobilization, absorptive capacity, knowledge base of management, and managerial capabilities (Jansen, Van den Bosch, & Volberda, 2005).

Flexibility is theoretically rooted in the areas of firm agility and change management (Sushil, 1999) and enterprise architecture and co-adaptation (Gromoff et al., 2012) and pursues innovation (Schumpeter, 1950) and competition (Grewal & Tanshuhaj, 2001). Equally essential but lacking attention is leadership behaviors that drive and facilitate flexibility and its dynamic impact on barriers to flexibility. Changing a core competency or value-added capability can demonstrably change a firm's strategic trajectory (Sanchez, 1996). With that in mind, firms can recoil; that is, firms can return to their core values and competencies, which is a positive intended consequence of flexibility. Change, *per se*, is an indefinite move away from a set of core competencies, especially if management intends not to return to those core competencies at a later future date.

This chapter establishes firm flexibility as *coiling and recoiling* of the firm's value emphasis, scope, attitude, etc. (i.e., once objectives have been met, the firm then retracts back to a core set of tenets, values, and competencies to meet the demands of a reconfigured business landscape). Flexibility, change, and leadership must, in this case, be seen as a triple bond needed for coiling and then recoiling flexibility within a given firm. All things related to the general idea of firm flexibility start at the helm of leadership. Thus, the following questions remain: Can entrepreneurial leadership most significantly overcome the barriers of flexibility within a given firm? Will entrepreneurial leadership impact organizational flexibility on three fronts: competitive, operations, and strategic?

There are three broad types of organizational flexibility: operational, competitive, and strategic (Sharma & Jain, 2010). Operational flexibility is such that any changes do not require significant shifts between the firm and its environment. Changes in terms of operational flexibility are temporary and not long-lasting or substantive. Competitive flexibility creates major changes and shifts in a firm's market position, such as introducing something new or novel to a market. Strategic flexibility, which is a consequence of a dynamic and radical new development, tends to be related to changes in the firm's environment. Because flexibility is a complex construct and has multipronged proclivities toward market changes, it is imperative to engage theoretical research questions about moves made by competitors and a firm's responses to competitors' moves and its environment. A given firm's market proclivities are related to creating new products, entering new markets, and maintaining a market position of stability (Sharma & Jain, 2010).

While there are other flexibilities (i.e., technical, financial, and marketing), it is likely that management and leadership are closer to the competitive, operational, and strategic organizational flexibility ranges of the firm. Leadership is significant concerning flexibility, particularly when flexibility is viewed as a transitionary process whereby the instability of the business landscape is in constant flux, which causes operational and strategic coiling and recoiling to maintain a competitive advantage and market position. However, with most things, operations and strategic tactics have certain degrees of obsolescence, which makes that very competitive advantage, in the long run, clearly a disadvantage when creating organizational inflexibility. At a deeper level, how is organizational flexibility shaped by leadership behaviors?

ter Hoeven and van Zoonen (2015) pointed to job design as having a significant effect on subordinate autonomy and spatial flexibility. Mendez, Howell, and Bishop (2015) sampled 28 committees and reported a correlation between leadership behaviors and performance. On the other hand, Schriesheim, Castro, Zhou, and DeChurch (2006) sampled 169 employees in 40 distinct groups and reported that a leader's perception of his or her behaviors is more significant than group members' observation effects of leadership behaviors. Silverthrone (2001) focused on managers' ability to change leadership behaviors based on changes in the business environment and whether it improved subordinates' performance over time.

Entrepreneurial Leadership, Attitudes, and Behavior Changes

To capture unintended opportunity, especially when the firm is faced with fierce competition, shared values between leadership and subordinates must be established to obtain and maintain a climate of high-velocity movements and knowledge acquisition. Values that are internally reexamined allow innovation and flexibility to flourish instead of a closed enterprise system that is unable to shift the emphasis on values in the face of competition, which eventually creates a forced rejection out of a given market (Ensign & Robinson, 2016).

Changing the emphasis on values, attitudes, and beliefs can be stymied when management values or devalues risk aversion. Tang and Rothenberg (2009) wrote, "Values evolve and become more conservative, risk-averse, and less dynamic as a firm transforms into a mature corporation" (p. 183). For this reason, Ensign and Robinson (2016) promoted two types of corporate entrepreneurs: *offensive* and *defensive*. Offensive and defensive entrepreneurial capabilities have consequential effects on the likely approach to organizational flexibility. One effect is the movement of values and perhaps an abrupt shift of interests; another effect is the challenge to preexisting values, processes, procedures, and structures (Ensign & Robinson, 2016).

According to Ensign and Robinson (2016), an offensive entrepreneurial climate creates an innovative environment where ideas can flourish, which extends to shifting values. This type of offensive entrepreneurship seems likely to support flexibility— flexibility that can make extensions, value adjustments, and return to an original state (i.e., the coiling and recoiling effect) at some point in time. Change of creative attitudes and behaviors to reach entrepreneurial goals must be adapted at some point in the firm's life cycle (Newman et al., 2018). In the same way, leaders who are entrepreneurial have abilities that distinguish them from non-entrepreneurial leaders whose differentiation resides in what Fernald et al. (2005) called the "entrepreneurial mentality" (p. 4). To take Fernald et al.'s position and ranking of flexibility as a common characteristic, it is leadership that supports flexibility from an enterprise perspective.

Newman et al. (2018) explained that entrepreneurism is the process whereby the leader influences subordinates to recognize and exploit opportunities toward entrepreneurial goals. Kuratko, Ireland, Covin, and Hornsby (2005) suggested that spontaneous and opportunity-seeking behaviors are inherent in any entrepreneurial pursuits within any given firm. Therefore, entrepreneurial leaders influence and motivate others to pursue entrepreneurial goals (Gupta, MacMillian, & Surie, 2004). If there are behaviors that entrepreneurial individuals, groups, and institutions possess, what are the patterns that persist in different marketplaces? Does the entrepreneurial mentality remain or adapt when exposed to different marketplaces or innovative opportunities in various firms? If it does, what is the pattern of flexibility in various industries and the leadership that influenced those adaptations?

Entrepreneurial leadership facilitates enterprise flexibility in that employees' behavior and attitude are affected by change (Soriano & Martinez, 2007). The benefit of entrepreneurial leadership is to affect subordinates' behavior and attitude toward positive change during new circumstances that require adaptivity and capability. It has been long established that when firms adhere to the constraining elements of institutional policy, resources, and procedures, entrepreneurial activity is stifled (Ensign & Robinson, 2016). Without adequate employee behavioral substitutes and modifications to facilitate enterprise change, flexibility is indefensible.

Therefore, entrepreneurial leadership *transmits* and *exchanges* knowledge and has the *know how* and the *how to* to change subordinates' attitudes and behaviors when faced with the many barriers to enterprise flexibility. It is theorized that entrepreneurial leadership transmission of values, knowledge, and beliefs will, in effect, decrease the barriers to enterprise flexibility. Bhardwaj and Momaya's (2006) salient case study on the effects of corporate entrepreneurship on organizational flexibility with an emphasis on the S-A-P analysis was first developed by Sushil (1997). The gap and limitation of their analysis was the explication of the *actor* who is henceforth described as an entrepreneur with attitudes and behaviors that other management/subordinates do not possess but that can be transmitted and exchanged to create competitive advantages.

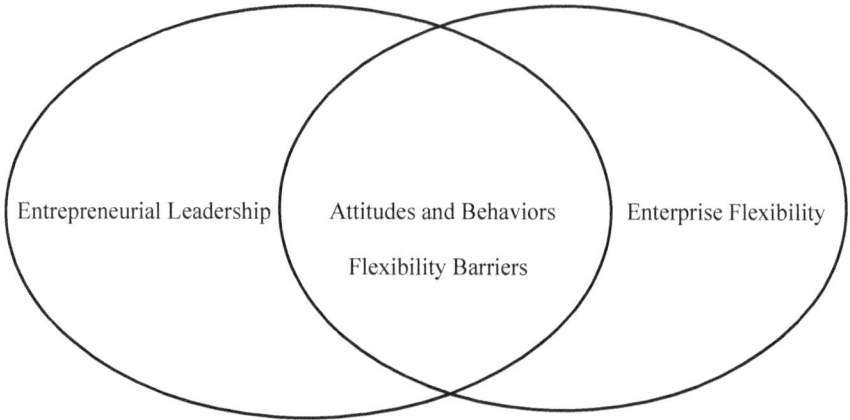

Figure 1. Entrepreneurial leadership as a catalyst for enterprise flexibility.

P₁: Entrepreneurial leadership significantly impacts
        subordinates' attitudes and work-related behaviors.

Entrepreneurial Leadership as the Catalyst for Enterprise Flexibility

Entrepreneurial leadership transmits tacit knowledge (e.g., the firm is a collection of knowledge) through the social environment—those very characteristics that they embody. Some of these characteristics are creators of novelty, independent, innovators, learners, optimizers of resources, optimistic, risk-takers, resourceful, and initiators (Landstrom, 1999). Enterprise flexibility at the firm level has barriers that require value-added activities to overcome the inertia established by the status quo of enterprise rigidity, such as the other barriers to flexibility outlined by Brozovic (2018). Brozovic's proposed barriers to flexibility are (a) rigidity, (b) management issues, (c) technology, (d) structural barriers, and (e) resistance to change. However, it does depend on the type of flexibility, which *ex ante* specifies correlative attitude, behavior, and value-added activities. Both Sushil (2000) and Volberda (1996) agreed that the attitudes and behaviors of those involved in flexibility (i.e., recoiling process) establish a supporting cast of group members whose mission is to create value-added activities within the constraints of a business model (Leitch & Volery, 2017).

The ability to transmit beliefs, knowledge, and values to subordinates resides in the characteristics of the entrepreneurial leaders themselves, whose knowledge and vision when transmitted to subordinates are significant enough to increase the chances of a shared vision that encompasses a future orientation or transformation within the business model (Gupta et al., 2004). Entrepreneurial leaders transmit beliefs and values *via* their vision (Ruvio, Rosenblatt, & Hertz-Lazarowitz, 2010); visions create the ideal mindset by comprising and incorporating stages in growth, innovation, and the creation toward a somewhat uncertain future, whereas a reactive and non-adaptive vision can have the opposite effects. Ensign and Robinson (2016) said, "Entrepreneurship will occur and succeed if previously held views and beliefs are abandoned" (p. 176).

P_2: Entrepreneurial leadership positively impacts organizational flexibility.

Entrepreneurial Leadership and Organizational Flexibility Barriers

Kuratko et al. (2007) described the entrepreneurial leader as possessing several characteristics associated with the *spirit* of the traditional entrepreneur: risk-taker, idea champion, and prime innovator, and innovative in the sense that they are at the cross-section of various functions with the firm's business strategy. Along with Kuratko et al.'s entrepreneurial leadership characteristics are a willingness to change direction, focus on long-term results, and the temperament to tolerate ambiguity (Balkin & Logan, 1988). According to Hentschke (2010), three characteristics embody entrepreneurial leaders: they have unique ideas, they raise capital (financial and social), and they seek business growth based on ideas. Cast and scenario enactment, including building commitments and specifying limits, are accomplished by entrepreneurial leaders by framing challenges, absorbing uncertainty, and clearing a path (Gupta et al., 2004).

Other factors related to the spirit of entrepreneurial leadership that get far less attention are the *external factors*, which also comprise those parties affiliated within strategic groups that directly and indirectly impact the fluidity of enterprise flexibility (Jones & Crompton, 2009). Volberda (1999) agreed, "It is hard to find managers who refer to their organizations as stable, orderly, and non-changing" (p. 17).

But, as known, entrepreneurial leaders do not work in silos but within a social setting—the organization; either way, there is a coordination of information and alertness of opportunity (Kirzner, 1999) that creates an imbalance toward a firm's competitive advantage or a disequilibrium (Schumpeter, 1950). However, the adjustment process concerning equilibrium has not been explored (Van Praag, 1999). Thus, the entrepreneurial leadership phenomenon falls within two categories: an internal venture or an internal group (i.e., intrapreneurship; Balkin & Logan, 1988). The firm can assume either category but will ultimately have to challenge interfirm rigidity (Kouropalatis et al., 2012; Singh, Singh Oberoi, & Singh Ahuja, 2013), lack of information (Shimizu & Hitt, 2004), resistance to change (Skordoulis, 2004), and cultural and structural barriers (Hickman, 1998; Volberda, 1999).

Interfirm rigidity, lack of information, resistance to change, and cultural and structural barriers are the most challenging obstacles to overcome within any organizational context. Taking these barriers into consideration, a firm has two options: be either proactive or reactive in the face of competitive pressures because *no action* is the worst option. Even the very notion of a reactive response to competition entails a level of flexibility (i.e., recoiling). That is, flexibility does not specify a direction of the firm's strategy, only that the core of the firm has shifted (or extended) in another unintended direction and, consequently, may return to its original core at a future date. However, the main idea here is to connect the core principles of entrepreneurial leadership that support firm flexibility with inherent barriers.

Entrepreneurial Leadership Supports Enterprise Flexibility

Tables 1 and 2 illustrate the constructs of entrepreneurial leadership and organizational flexibility. Each construct's dimensions are associative, but that does not imply a one-to-one correlation. One of the strongest leadership characteristics is a leader's vision, regardless of if the vision was conceptualized either in the entrepreneurial mindset or collectively. It is not a surprise that entrepreneurial leaders use vision to share and gain information between groups and units as a decentralizing mechanism, thereby decreasing boundaries and allowing information to flow within the firm. This is a critical component of how entrepreneurial leaders are effective even if most of the operations are automated, whereby the entrepreneurial vision and problem solving are critical in the context of an advisor or coordinator (Coulson-Thomas, 2015), or even applicable in enterprise architecture (Gromoff et al., 2012).

Table 1

Flexible Barriers Explained

Flexible Barrier	Description
Internal rigidity	Preference of a status quo; negative contribution to performance; maladaptation to existing or future market changes
Lack of information	Lacking environment know-how; unaware of the level of uncertainty; starts with the fear of the unknown; established routines; inability to reverse seemingly poor decisions; harsh on mistakes
Resistance to change	Closed versus open systems; difficulty coping with business cycles; organizational reservations
Structural and cultural barriers	Organizational survival is attained when matched to the environment; an organization can adapt to its resources or to the norms and beliefs of an environment; organizations can be prisoners of their past, which disables future changes.

Adapted from "Strategic Flexibility: A Review of the Literature," by D. Brozovic, 2018, *International Journal of Management Reviews, 20*(1), 3-31.

Table 2

Entrepreneurial Leadership Dimensions

Leadership Dimension	Description
Vision	"A vision is formulated by explicitly identifying a domain for competitive behavior, a set of sources of competitive strength, and a profile for resource capability."
Problem-solving	"Effective leadership must solve, or face, problems quickly and forcefully, regardless of their nature."
Decision-making	"Whether leaders are directive or supportive, they know they must make decisions that commit the organization to critical actions."
Risk-taking	"Leaders must weigh the multitudinous factors involved while understanding that no one can predict the future with certainty."
Strategic initiatives	"Leadership, strategies, and structure will reflect entrepreneurial thinking with associated characteristics, e.g., a problem-solving and action orientation."

Adapted from "A New Paradigm: Entrepreneurial Leadership," by L. W. Fernald, G. T. Solomon, & A. Tarabishy, 2005, *Southern Business Review*, *30*(2), 1-10.

Conceived from entrepreneurship (Kirzner, 1999; Schumpeter, 1950) are entrepreneurial types that discover and exploit market opportunities and who are alert to options that drive opportunistic choices. Entrepreneurial types possess a level of universal awareness of opportunities within the firm. Without having entrepreneurial types in the firm to discover and innovate results in poor alignment and rigid perspectives and rigid organizational structure. There is a strong connection between information leading to knowledge and the interfirm entrepreneurial capabilities.

Why is there a lack of information, and how does a lack of information bottleneck the firm's market change opportunities when attempting to respond to market changes? In many cases, a firm's attempts to change are first considered from a strategic perspective because flexibility is costly and evokes employee resistance (Coulson-Thomas, 2015). Entrepreneurial leadership enables flexibility through decision-making with a commitment to the objective, which is vital when the firm *encounters threats* that were unforeseen and/or when in the pursuit of new business models (Sharma & Jain, 2010). Entrepreneurial leadership was reported to be significantly related to enterprise performance during mergers and acquisitions primarily because of the influence, vision, and decision-making qualities of this type of leader during transitional times of chaos and ambiguity (Strobl, Bauer, & Matzler, 2018).

A lack of organizational flexibility is associated with rigidity in decision-making and, thus, associated with maintaining the status quo. Any leadership team, particularly a new top management team or new strategic leadership, has approximately 180 days (6 months) before the tyranny of the status quo sets in and no changes can be effectively made (Friedman & Friedman, 1984). While it may sound optimistic that only entrepreneurial leaders drive flexibility and are the motivators of subordinates, evidently their role is critical in disrupting the tyranny of the status quo. The disruptive connotation of entrepreneurial leadership moves the enterprise away from a state of rigidity by employing value-added capabilities, embracing serendipity across all levels of the enterprise, and maintaining high levels of alertness to advance unforeseen opportunities. Non-entrepreneurial leaders do not foresee the detrimental effects of the status quo on concentrated areas of enterprise performance. However, the benefits from entrepreneurial leadership when serendipity arises or emerges from a business strategy will need to be cultivated and influenced by entrepreneurial leadership and subordinates to achieve the value of flexibility.

Depending on the various forms of strategy-making, one can provide further evidence that strategic initiative as an entrepreneurial leadership dimension will challenge the firm's internal barriers that disable flexibility. Barbuto (2016) described strategy-making processes as autocratic, transformative, rational, or political, depending on the complexity of the firm and desire for a specific type of leadership approach.

Mintzberg and Waters (1985) designated eight types of strategic approaches: (a) planned, (b) entrepreneurial, (c) ideological, (d) umbrella, (e) process, (f) unconnected, (g) consensus, and (h) imposed. Each of these strategic types has an embedded consequence that results in *change* and *flexibility* and that is initiated by either the entrepreneurial leader or a team of entrepreneurial leaders. This type of leadership tendentiously comports with action and is a prerequisite of influence that originates from an entrepreneurial mindset. Out of these eight strategy types, seven originate from and are formulated by leadership. Most compelling are the descriptors and illustrations where entrepreneurial leadership plays a central role in both determining the type of strategy and how it is shaped.

For example, the entrepreneurial strategy type starts as an individualized, unarticulated vision from leadership. The intention of an entrepreneurial type of strategy is that it allows for what emerges. Conversely, a planned strategy, albeit not known for its entrepreneurial spirit, typifies the process of planning that is inherent in the formulation of planning the use of resources. The process of planning establishes a series of the formalized plans to confirm the strategy as *surprise-free*; that is, the strategy is and will be constrained by an initially conceptualized direction of preplanned goals, including managerial controls to hone them in. This approach is codified under the auspice of a constrained approach, which is ineffective in a competitive landscape driven by emerging market demands, competitive pressures, and new circumstances of the firm.

Objectives of the Study

The main objective of this study is to theoretically examine and connect entrepreneurial leadership and organizational flexibility theories. Neither theory has been examined or tested on the interaction and consequential effects within and between firms. This is a purely theoretical attempt to set the stage for further research by providing research questions and postulates. Research questions and postulates emerge from the vast amount of prior research studies. Three postulates are provided based on the interaction between entrepreneurial leadership and organizational flexibility in this new framework:

P₃: Entrepreneurial leadership positively impacts operational flexibility.

P₄: Entrepreneurial leadership positively impacts competitive flexibility.

P₅: Entrepreneurial leadership positively impacts on strategic flexibility.

This study reviewed prior research studies to develop a new conceptual framework. This literature was employed to develop a new theoretical framework that explains the interaction and consequential effects of entrepreneurial leadership and organizational flexibility. Following a review of the literature, a set of postulates and research questions was formed for profitable future research endeavors. Studies were culled based on their inclusion of the following keywords: management, strategic management, the flexibility of the firm, and entrepreneurial studies (theory and application).

CONCLUSION

As a matter of course, prior research findings help establish *a priori* research questions and postulates within this new conceptual framework that can later be tested and examined by future researchers *a posteriori*. The following five research questions extrapolated from this examination need to be quantitatively examined in future research:

RQ₁: Entrepreneurial leadership has a significant impact on subordinates' attitudes and work-related behaviors?

RQ₂: Entrepreneurial leadership has a positive impact on organizational flexibility?

RQ₃: Entrepreneurial leadership has a positive impact on operational flexibility?

RQ₄: Entrepreneurial leadership has a positive impact on competitive flexibility?

RQ₅: Entrepreneurial leadership has a positive impact on strategic flexibility?

What has been established as theoretical contributions are innumerable to the flexibility and entrepreneurial leadership literature. These contributions to the literature claim that entrepreneurial leadership could potentially be associated with and/or facilitate those attitudes and behaviors required for organizational flexibility. In a similar vein, linking entrepreneurial leadership characteristics to overcome the barriers to enterprise flexibility is a much-required injection of entrepreneurial leadership. Indeed, the connection between entrepreneurial leadership and organizational flexibility needs to be tested empirically. Entrepreneurial leadership positively influences strategy implementation, change management, and performance (Adler, Goldoftas, & Levine, 1999). To date, there is sparse empirical evidence to confirm the positive effects of entrepreneurial leadership on organizational flexibility, performance, and a firm's adaptation to change (incremental, radical, etc.) so that determinates of entrepreneurial leadership can be understood, because as it stands, the results are limited.

The limited amount of empirical evidence connecting these constructs no doubt leaves several gaps in the literature. The current chapter attempts to ignite an increasingly important dialogue that informs how entrepreneurial leadership supports any variation of enterprise flexibility. In this regard, entrepreneurial leaders are creators of new and novel paths of inductive strategic initiatives; however, they also carry out deductive strategic initiatives based on pre-established objectives that involve an entrepreneurial mindset (Kuratko et al., 2007; Mintzberg & Westley, 1992). Entrepreneurial leadership influences others to act on new ideas and search for exploitation and discovery while not being overtly innovative *per se*. The challenge for entrepreneurial leadership is to direct market change that is revolutionary, isolated, incremental, or focused.

Entrepreneurial leaders influence flexibility (i.e., recoiling) by viewing competitive tactics as *outsiders*—those who have the capability to challenge future uncertainty and have a vastly different perspective—or as *insiders* (Ensign & Robinson, 2016).

Henry Ford found and hired employees who were gifted *tinkerers*, many of whom were direct contributors and were duly attributed to some of the most significant innovations of the 20th century (Zunz, 1992). Characterizing Ford's tinkerers as entrepreneurial leaders of his day, Zunz said it was the constant "exchange of ideas that led to innovation" (p. 87). At the convergence of vision, influence, and transformational decision-making, entrepreneurial leadership is an effective type of leadership but needs more theoretical development.

Henceforth, the development of the entrepreneur can be traced as far back as Richard Cantillon's conceptualization of the entrepreneur as the market mechanism, Schumpeter's *disequilibrium*. Abbe' Nicolas Baudeau's entrepreneur was the inventor and/or innovator who created profit under uncertainty; even Jean-Baptiste Say added that his entrepreneur (in his *Cours Complet d'Ecomnie Politique Pratique*) methodically employs three steps: the attainment of certain knowledge, the ability to apply that particular knowledge, and the ability to realize a product from that application (Hébert & Link, 1982).

From an Austrian School perspective, there is a leadership quality that is coupled with an entrepreneurial disposition that orients one toward organization and positive influence of a firm's factors of production (Salerno, 2008). Entrepreneurial leadership is a competitive synthesizer; this type of leadership notices opportunities on the horizon that others are unable to notice (Kirzner, 1997). This type of leadership also supports the recoiling cycle (i.e., reflexibility) as a firm's value emphasis shifts according to market changes, being extended, and then retracted to return to core competencies. For example, management is encouraged to shift the value emphasis and increase flexibility because of market signals. To address market signals, management can either make routine or non-routine decisions; non-routine decisions require a high level of strategic thinking that is entrepreneurial in nature (Child, 2015; Gross, 2016). Entrepreneurially driven firms are primed to be more alert to market signals and can employ flexibility on a temporal or intertemporal basis. Perhaps firms can be elastically flexible in that they extend, and contract based on resources and on a less extreme basis in terms of the level of intended flexibility and uncertain market conditions.

A flexible cycle and elastic entrepreneurial function would increase the level of uncertainty but would also increase the entrepreneurial behaviors in the firm and provide an agile intertemporal transition of resources to assert short-term market competitiveness. Thus, entrepreneurial leadership should not be viewed as a one-person army or "leadership by informed consent" (Hickman, 1998, p. 196). However, there are individual factors that come into play in determining effectiveness in the pursuit of flexibility (i.e., competitive flexibility, strategic flexibility, and operational flexibility). Employees (entrepreneurial or non-entrepreneurial) are aware of the constrained or unconstrained nature of the firm; often, however, they already have an end in mind but are without the means to set forth on an entrepreneurial trajectory. Entrepreneurial decision-making and strategic thinking are significant components of a firm's operational system. A strong climate of entrepreneurial leadership, which has many advantages, serves as an interorganizational catalyst to overcome organizational barriers, and take advantage of organizational flexibility.

FUTURE RESEARCH

The scope of future research in this vineyard must focus on the consequential effects of entrepreneurial leadership on strategic flexibility and its relation to time. The research focus needs to examine these effects at both the firm level and individual level of analysis in order to determine which is the most flexible: the firm, the market, or the individual. It is in this vein that future research must proceed. Future endeavors should be quantitative as well as qualitative, with a focus on intertemporal effects.

REFERENCES

Adler, P. S., Goldoftas, B., & Levine, D. I. (1999). Flexibility versus efficiency? A case study of model changeovers in the Toyota production system. *Organization Science*, *10*(1), 43-68.

Antonakis, J., & Autio, E. (2007). Entrepreneurship and leadership. *The Psychology of Entrepreneurship*, 189-207.

Atkinson, J. (1985). *Flexibility, uncertainty and manpower management* (No. 89). Brighton, UK: Institute of Manpower Studies.

Balkin, D. B., & Logan, J. W. (1988). Reward policies that support entrepreneurship. *Compensation & Benefits Review*, *20*(1), 18-25.

Barbuto, J. E., Jr. (2016). How is strategy formed in organizations? A multi-disciplinary taxonomy of strategy-making approaches. *Journal of Behavioral and Applied Management*, *3*(1), 822.

Bass, B. M., & Avolio, B. J. (1994). Transformational leadership and organizational culture. *The International Journal of Public Administration*, *17*(3-4), 541-554.

Bhardwaj, B. R., & Momaya, K. (2006). Role of organizational flexibility for corporate entrepreneurship: Case study of FedEx Corporation. *Global Journal of Flexible Systems Management*, 7(1/2), 37-44.

Brozovic, D. (2018). Strategic flexibility: A review of the literature. *International Journal of Management Reviews*, *20*(1), 3-31.

Carlsson, B. (1999). Small business, entrepreneurship, and industrial dynamics. In Z. Acs & S. Ackerman (Eds.), *Are small firms important? Their role and impact* (pp. 99-110). Boston, MA: Springer.

Child, J. (2015). *Organization: Contemporary principles and practice*. Oxford, UK: Blackwell.

Chowdary, B. V. (2001). Flexibility and related issues in evaluation and selection of technological systems. *Global Journal of Flexible Systems Management, 2*(2), 11-20.

Coulson-Thomas, C. (2015). Leadership, innovation and business growth. *Management Services, 60*(2), 36-43.

De Groote, X. (1994). The flexibility of production processes: A general framework. *Management Science, 40*(7), 933-945.

Ensign, P. C., & Robinson, N. P. (2016). Offensive and defensive corporate entrepreneurship: Learning to think like an outsider. *Journal of Enterprising Culture, 24*(02), 169-191.

Fernald, L. W., Solomon, G. T., & Tarabishy, A. (2005). A new paradigm: Entrepreneurial leadership. *Southern Business Review, 30*(2), 1-10.

Friedman, M., & Friedman, R. D. (1984). *Tyranny of the status quo*. Orlando, FL: Harcourt Brace Co.

Grewal, R., & Tanshuhaj, P. (2001). Building organizational capabilities for managing economic crisis: The role of market orientation and strategic flexibility. *Journal of Marketing, 65*, 67-80.

Gromoff, A., Kazantsev, N., Kozhevnikov, D., Ponfilenok, M., & Stavenko, Y. (2012). Newer approach to create flexible business architecture of modern enterprise. *Global Journal of Flexible Systems Management, 13*(4), 207-215.

Gross, R. (2016). Towards an understanding of the relationship between leadership styles and strategic thinking: A small and medium enterprise perspective. *Journal of Business Studies Quarterly, 8*(2), 22-39.

Gross, R. (2019). The nexus between followership and entrepreneurial leadership: A firm-level analysis. *Journal of Management Policy and Practice, 20*(5).

Gupta, V., MacMillan, I. C., & Surie, G. (2004). Entrepreneurial leadership: Developing and measuring a cross-cultural construct. *Journal of Business Venturing, 19*(2), 241-260.

Handy, C. (1995). Trust and the virtual organization. *Long Range Planning, 28*(4), 126-126.

Hébert, R. F., & Link, A. N. (1982). *The entrepreneur: Mainstream views and radical critiques.* New York, NY: Praeger.

Hentschke, G. C. (2010). Developing entrepreneurial leaders. In B. Davies & M. Brundrett (Eds.), *Developing successful leadership* (pp. 115-132). Dordrecht, The Netherlands: Springer.

Hickman, G. R. (1998). *Leading organizations: Perspectives for a new era.* Thousand Oaks, CA. Sage.

Hmieleski, K. M., & Ensley, M. D. (2007). A contextual examination of new venture performance: Entrepreneur leadership behavior, top management team heterogeneity, and environmental dynamism. *Journal of Organizational Behavior, 28*(7), 865-889.

Jansen, J. J., Van den Bosch, F. A., & Volberda, H. W. (2005). Exploratory innovation, exploitative innovation, and ambidexterity: The impact of environmental and organizational antecedents. *Schmalenbach Business Review, 57*(4), 351-363.

Jones, O., & Crompton, H. (2009). Enterprise logic and small firms: A model of authentic entrepreneurial leadership. *Journal of Strategy and Management, 2*(4), 329-351.

Kanter, R. M. (1983). *The change masters: Innovation for productivity in the American mode.* New York, NY: Simon and Schuster.

Kanter, R. M. (1994). Collaborative advantage. *Harvard Business Review, 72*(4), 96-108.

Kirzner, I. M. (1973). *Competition & entrepreneurship.* Chicago, IL: University of Chicago Press.

Kirzner, I. M. (1997). Entrepreneurial discovery and the competitive market process: An Austrian approach. *Journal of Economic Literature, 35*(1), 60-85.

Kirzner, I. M. (1999). Creativity and/or alertness: A reconsideration of the Schumpeterian entrepreneur. *The Review of Austrian Economics, 11*(1-2), 5-17.

Knight, F. H. (1933). *Risk, uncertainty and profit*. New York, NY: Houghton Mifflin Co.

Kouropalatis, Y., Hughes, P., & Morgan, R. E. (2012). Pursuing "flexible commitment" as strategic ambidexterity: An empirical justification in high technology firms. *European Journal of Marketing, 46*(10), 1389-1417.

Kuratko, D. F., Hornsby, J. S., & Goldsby, M. G. (2007). The relationship of stakeholder salience, organizational posture, and entrepreneurial intensity to corporate entrepreneurship. *Journal of Leadership & Organizational Studies, 13*(4), 56-72.

Kuratko, D. F., Ireland, R. D., Covin, J. G., & Hornsby, J. S. (2005). A model of middle-level managers' entrepreneurial behavior. *Entrepreneurship Theory and Practice, 29*(6), 699-716.

Landstrom, H. (1999). The roots of entrepreneurship research. *New England Journal of Entrepreneurship, 2*(2), 9.

Leibenstein, H. (1968). Entrepreneurship and development. *The American Economic Review, 58*(2), 72-83.

Leitch, C. M., & Volery, T. (2017). Entrepreneurial leadership: Insights and directions. *International Small Business Journal, 35*(2), 147-156.

Mendez, M. J., Howell, J. P., & Bishop, J. W. (2015). Beyond the unidimensional collective leadership model. *Leadership & Organization Development Journal, 36*(6), 675-696.

Mintzberg, H. (1989). *Mintzberg on management: Inside our strange world of organizations*. New York, NY: Free Press.

Mintzberg, H. (1990). The design school: Reconsidering the basic premises of strategic management. *Strategic Management Journal, 11*(3), 171-195.

Mintzberg, H., & Waters, J. A. (1985). Of strategies, deliberate and emergent. *Strategic Management Journal, 6*(3), 257-272.

Mintzberg, H., & Westley, F. (1992). Cycles of organizational change. *Strategic Management Journal, 13*(S2), 39-59.

Mises, L. V. (1949). Profit and loss. In *Planning for Freedom* (pp. 108-150.) Auburn, AL: Mises Institute.

Newman, A., Herman, H. M., Schwarz, G., & Nielsen, I. (2018). The effects of employees' creative self-efficacy on innovative behavior: The role of entrepreneurial leadership. *Journal of Business Research, 89,* 1-9.

Northouse, P. G. (2007). *Leadership: Theory and practice.* Thousand Oaks, CA: Sage.

Parnell, J. A. (2005). Strategic philosophy and management level. *Management Decision, 43*(2), 157-170.

Peters, T. J. (1987). *Thriving on chaos: Handbook for a Management Revolution.* New York, NY: Harper and Row.

Renko, M., El Tarabishy, A., Carsrud, A. L., & Brännback, M. (2015). Understanding and measuring entrepreneurial leadership style. *Journal of Small Business Management, 53*(1), 54-74.

Roberts, N., & Stockport, G. J. (2009). Defining strategic flexibility. *Global Journal of Flexible Systems Management, 10*(1), 27-32.

Rodgers, C. S. (1992). The flexible workplace: What have we learned? *Human Resource Management, 31*(3), 183-199.

Roomi, M. A., & Harrison, P. (2011). Entrepreneurial leadership: What is it and how should it be taught? *International Review of Entrepreneurship, 9*(3), 1-44.

Rothbard, M. N. (1985). Professor Hébert on entrepreneurship. *Journal of Libertarian Studies, 7*(2), 281-286.

Ruvio, A., Rosenblatt, Z., & Hertz-Lazarowitz, R. (2010). Entrepreneurial leadership vision in nonprofit vs. for-profit organizations. *The Leadership Quarterly, 21*(1), 144-158.

Salerno, J. T. (2008). The entrepreneur: Real and imagined. *The Quarterly Journal of Austrian Economics, 11*(3-4), 188-207.

Sanchez, R. (1996). Strategic product creation: Managing new interactions of technology, markets, and organizations. *European Management Journal, 14*(2), 121-138.

Schriesheim, C. A., Castro, S. L., Zhou, X. T., & DeChurch, L. A. (2006). An investigation of path-goal and transformational leadership theory predictions at the individual level of analysis. *The Leadership Quarterly, 17*(1), 21-38.

Schumpeter, J. A. (1934). *The theory of economic development: An inquiry into profits, capital, credit, interest, and the business cycle*. Cambridge, MA: Harvard University Press.

Schumpeter, J. (1950). The process of creative destruction. In J. Schumpeter (Ed.), *Capitalism, socialism and democracy* (3rd ed., pp. 131-145). London, England: Allen and Unwin.

Scott, W. R., & Meyer, J. W. (1994). *Institutional environments and organizations: Structural complexity and individualism.* Thousand Oaks, CA: Sage.

Shane, S., & Venkataraman, S. (2000). The promise of entrepreneurship as a field of research. *Academy of Management Review, 25*(1), 217-226.

Sharma, M. K., & Jain, P. K. (2010). Revisiting flexibility in organizations: Exploring its impact on performance. *Global Journal of Flexible Systems Management, 11*(3), 51-68.

Shimizu, K., & Hitt, M. A. (2004). Strategic flexibility: Organizational preparedness to reverse ineffective strategic decisions. *Academy of Management Perspectives, 18*(4), 44-59.

Silverthorne, C. (2001). Leadership effectiveness and personality: A cross-cultural evaluation. *Personality and Individual Differences, 30*(2), 303-309.

Singh, D., Singh Oberoi, J., & Singh Ahuja, I. (2013). An empirical investigation of dynamic capabilities in managing strategic flexibility in manufacturing organizations. *Management Decision, 51*(7), 1442-1461.

Skordoulis, R. T. (2004). Strategic flexibility and change: An aid to strategic thinking or another managerial abstraction? *Strategic Change, 13*(5), 253-258.

Soriano, D. R., & Martínez, J. M. C. (2007). Transmitting the entrepreneurial spirit to the work team in SMEs: The importance of leadership. *Management Decision, 45*(7), 1102-1122.

Steers, R. M. (1975). Problems in the measurement of organizational effectiveness. *Administrative Science Quarterly*, 546-558.

Strobl, A., Bauer, F., & Matzler, K. (2018). The impact of industry-wide and target market environmental hostility on entrepreneurial leadership in mergers and acquisitions. *Journal of World Business, 55*(2).

Surie, G., & Ashley, A. (2008). Integrating pragmatism and ethics in entrepreneurial leadership for sustainable value creation. *Journal of Business Ethics, 81*(1), 235-246.

Sushil, S. (1997). Flexible systems management: An evolving paradigm. *Systems Research Behavioral Science, 14*(4), 259-275.

Sushil. S. (1999). *Flexibility in management: Global institute of flexible systems management*. New Delhi, India: Vikas Publishing House.

Sushil, S. (2000). Concept of systemic flexibility. *Global Journal of Flexible Systems Management, 1*(1), 77-88.

Sushil, S. (2001). Demythifying flexibility. *Management Decision, 39*(10), 860-865.

Tang, Z., & Rothenberg, S. (2009). Does perceptual acuity matter? An investigation of entrepreneurial orientation, perceptual acuity, and firm performance. *Journal of Enterprising Culture, 17*(01), 79-102.

ter Hoeven, C. L., & van Zoonen, W. (2015). Flexible work designs and employee well-being: Examining the effects of resources and demands. *New Technology, Work and Employment, 30*(3), 237-255.

van der Weerdt, N. P., Volberda, H. W., Verwaal, E., & Stienstra, M. (2012). Organizing for flexibility: Addressing dynamic capabilities and organization design. In A. Bøllingtoft, L. Donaldson, G. P. Huber, D. D. Håkonsson, & C. C. Snow (Eds.), *Collaborative communities of firms* (pp. 105-125). New York, NY: Springer.

Van Praag, C. M. (1999). Some classic views on entrepreneurship. *De Economist, 147*(3), 311-335.

Volberda, H. W. (1996). Toward the flexible form: How to remain vital in hypercompetitive environments. *Organization Science, 7*(4), 359-374.

Volberda, H. W. (1998). *Toward the flexible form: How to remain vital in hypercompetitive environments.* In A. Y. Ilinitch, A. Y. Lewin, & R. D'Aveni (Eds.), Managing in times of disorder: Hyper competitive organizational responses (pp. 267-296). Thousand Oaks, CA: Sage.

Volberda, H. W. (1999). *Building the flexible firm: How to remain competitive.* New York, NY: Oxford University Press.

Yukl, G. (2009). Leading organizational learning: Reflections on theory and research. *The Leadership Quarterly, 20*(1), 49-53.

Zunz, O. (1992). *Making America corporate 1870-1920.* Chicago, IL: University of Chicago Press.

Chapter 5:
Strategy, Innovation, and Absorptive Capacity

This chapter explores strategic and entrepreneurial literature and presents a theoretical model purporting the moderating role of absorptive capacity (ACAP) at the organizational level of entrepreneurial orientation (EO). Strategic thinking and innovative behavior (IB) at the firm level are unexamined with a moderating influence. In a practical sense, this research presents opportunities to conceptualize ACAP on firm-level potential and realized capabilities.

This research develops a theoretical model that provides new testable linkages between constructs that have gone untested in strategic and entrepreneurial literature. It is proposed that ACAP moderates the relationship between strategic thinking and IB, producing a potentially stronger and significant impact on firm-level EO, thereby creating firm-level climates cultivating strategic behaviors. This exploratory research and theoretical model provide three proposals for future exploration and research consideration.

INTRODUCTION

Small and large enterprises create and often survive constant environmental change through structural reengineering due to insidious and/or known competitive forces in the business landscape. These insidious external forces pressure firms by the rapid speed in which they need to bring products to market, fast-moving market responses needed to develop comparative advantages through new knowledge acquisitions internally, and capitalization of the external knowledge base needed to enhance strategic positioning. These activities are not isolated to the individual employee. Rather, it is the entrepreneurial spirit executed internally.

Schumpeter, Galunic and Rodan (1998) emphasized, "The entrepreneur did not have to be a single individual but rather that the 'entrepreneurial function' was a social and co-operative process" (p. 3). Acquiring a new knowledge base externally and internally assimilating knowledge hinges on existing processes and structure so that managers and employees can embed it into the organizational structure for further commercialization. This has implications on the firm-level EO mechanisms, which ought not to be viewed axiomatically. The current research examines the literature to determine how ACAP, as a moderator, influences the relationship between strategic thinking and IB on firm-level EO. This research develops a theoretical model based on the knowledge-based view of the firm. The central question that prompts this research follows: Can externally acquired knowledge, when acquired by firm members and fused with internal knowledge, be strategically and innovatively assimilated, exploited, and commercialized, and does it increase or decrease firm-level EO?

EO has been tested with IB (Gross & Cabanda, 2016) and is related to strategic thinking (Gross, 2016b; Jelenc & Pisapia, 2015) at the individual level, but it has not been tested at the firm level. Previous studies related to the knowledge-based view of organizations have not emphasized the role and importance of cognitive factors and the requisite combination of value-added activities for firm-level strategy.

Barney, Wright, and Ketchen (2001) asked whether entrepreneurial firms were equipped with strategic cognitive abilities to identify and exploit market opportunities. The idea is to explicate the role of external knowledge and its purpose in continuous learning as a catalyst in entrepreneurial behaviors used to spot better emerging opportunities (Barney et al., 2001) and to develop the capability to harness knowledge spillovers that drive IB across industries (Malmberg & Maskell, 2002). Malmberg and Maskell (2002) expressed, "A local industrial structure with many firms competing in the same industry or collaborating across related industries tends to trigger processes which create not only dynamism and flexibility in general, but also learning and innovation" (p. 433).

The external environment is the ecosystem in which competitors vie for market share to enhance product and service positioning through acquiring and assimilating new knowledge. The current theoretical research intends to explore these relationships between strategic thinking, IB, and EO when moderated by ACAP while controlling for firm size, employee experience, and industry type.

This research is a salient addition to theory as there is scarce literature that focuses on the moderating effects of ACAP in the entrepreneurial context (Birdi, Leach, & Magadley, 2016), such as employee outbound activities pertaining to firm efficiency (Hughes & Wareham, 2010) and the process of IB based on the internalization of external knowledge, both of which are critical to theory development. To reinforce the saliency of this juncture, Easterby-Smith, Graça, Antonacopoulou, and Ferdinand (2008) said, "Few studies have examined the internal processes of absorptive capacity" (p. 484; see also Jansen, Van den Bosch, & Volberda, 2005).

Henceforth, the practical and theoretical implications that motivate this research are modeled to show how strategic behaviors evoke firm performance and influence firm strategy and competitive advantages. Strategic behaviors (i.e., strategic thinking and IB) remain the peripheral areas of strategy-making. That is, small and large enterprises develop products on a smaller scale when compared with large corporations and find themselves directly linked to the end consumer; therefore, owner decision-making and customer heterogeneity require efficient strategic-thinking capabilities, IB, and an entrepreneurial spirit to drive performance and to increase market share (Ebben & Johnson, 2005).

Accordingly, IB is an individual capability that manifests itself within the organization and is used as a competitive mechanism when cultivated by leadership (Gross, 2016a). IB manifests when a new product or internal practice is adopted without word-of-mouth benefit (Burns, 1987, 2007). For example, adopting new products and services based on shareholders' and competitors' experience and knowledge does not necessarily constitute that one's IB has been deployed. Nor would it suggest that strategic thinking was employed.

The mere process of adopting a product or service does not establish a culture of innovation (Burns, 2007). Stock, Greis, and Fischer (2001) agreed, "Empirical research that specifically examines the relationship between absorptive capacity and product development is limited and provides little direct guidance for the specific relationships" (p. 80). With the ever-increasing need for business enterprises to innovate rapidly and incrementally at the firm level, there is a resurgence of research needed to specify the antecedents of IB and determinates when influenced by ACAP. The current research emphasizes the internal manifestation of strategic thinking and the requisite external knowledge needed to fulfill interrelated firm processes based on the moderating role of ACAP. At the crux of ACAP are the two dimensions—potential capabilities and realized capabilities—that are noticeably the most critical due to their ethos of innovation (Cohen & Levinthal, 1990).

However, there is a strong consensus as to the ethos of IB (Burns, 2007; De Jong & Den Hartog, 2007; Gross, 2016a; Kleysen & Street, 2001; Roehrich, 2004; West & Farr, 1989) as the action taken by individuals, groups, and or teams for the generation and application of ideas toward a new product, service, or process that results in a novel discovery at any stage of the firm. What is absent in the IB literature is examining the underlying forces that allow employees to initiate IB based on external knowledge; this area is still unclear, segmented, and incomplete (Birdi et al., 2016). To add, strategic thinking is an individual mode of thinking that converges internal and external realities and directly and indirectly supports a firm's processes, products, services, and situational contexts. Jelenc, Pisapia, and Ivanusic (2015) explained, "Whenever unexpected events and/or research findings happen, people see it either because of the supremacy of strategic thinking or its lack of" (p. 7).

In the proceeding sections, this theoretical development creates a clearer understanding of the possible role of ACAP's moderating effect on employee EO; this notion reinforces the position held by Hughes and Wareham (2010), who considered ACAP akin to the outside-in process, where knowledge acquired externally should be relevant and applicable to the current position strategy related to internal capabilities. Knowledge acquisition occurs inside and outside the business landscape, although internal management ethos normally disallows fungible knowledge that could disrupt previously formulated directions. When knowledge is acquired, decisions should be made regarding how and where it will fit and the linkages of internal processes. Further, once triggered by knowledge acquired externally and assimilated internally, employees' outcomes might have considerable impacts on upper-echelon strategic consideration if management has an ethos of EO. Simply put, when managers receive newly acquired knowledge from the external environment, how does ACAP moderate the relationship between strategic behaviors and EO?

Past studies on EO employed hierarchical regression analysis and controlled for firm size, employees' experience, and industry type (Calantone, Schmidt, & Di Benedetto, 1997; Droge & Calantone, 1996; Stock et al., 2001; Tsai, 2001). The controlled variables could have strong spurious effects because each individual and organization has various degrees of differentiation in strategic direction, allocation of resources, and knowledge-based resources.

For example, where and how the knowledge is obtained and the method by which it is absorbed into the network causes paucity; however, it is important to understand that despite the size of the firm and one's experience, most businesses are not innovating in isolation but are building networks of shared knowledge across many business landscapes. The current research is unlike other studies that have focused on the type of knowledge imported into the enterprise (Vega-Jurado, Gutiérrez-Gracia, & Fernández-de-Lucio, 2009) or the strategies used to acquire new knowledge imported into the enterprise (Cassiman & Veugelers, 2006). This research explores how knowledge is used based on two explanatory factors and the moderating role of ACAP and its effect on firm-level entrepreneurial risks, innovativeness, and proactiveness. The current study presents three research propositions:

P1: Strategic thinking has a positive relationship with EO when moderated by ACAP.

P2: IB has a positive relationship with EO when moderated by ACAP.

P3: Strategic thinking and IB are positively related to EO.

The literature review provides a stream of research using an exploratory methodology with keywords germane to the research agenda and framework. This review aims to assist in developing theory. The possibilities of results rest on the moderating effects of ACAP.

LITERATURE REVIEW

Knowledge-Based View of the Firm

Strategy development is preceded by an active thrust of strategic ideas transmuted into tangible artifacts using capabilities based on individual competencies of knowledge-based internal networks; this is known as the *knowledge-based view of the firm* (Sveiby, 2001). This view of the firm is important because it explains how knowledge is generated, transferred, improved, and extended in the development of individual competence, ideas, and relationships, and it doubles as a managerial feedback mechanism (Allee, 2000). As knowledge is used internally and transferred through the apparatuses of the internal structure, it grows and expands and becomes a utility; conversely, when knowledge is stagnant, it depreciates and loses value (Sveiby, 2001). Every time knowledge is transferred between individuals, it replicates (Nonaka & Takeuchi, 1995), is converted, and then ameliorates individuals, workgroups, and work teams and enhances the general climate of the organization. The knowledge transferred within the firm's structure is intangible, inimitable, and a competitive resource (Grant, 1996; Sveiby, 2001).

Knowledge is not only a competitive resource, but it equips individuals to pursue strategic action at the most opportune time. As the business landscape changes, it adds to the level and sophistication of firm predictability. Knowledge is viewed as intangible and an enabling support apparatus that connects the internal firm environment and the external environment (Sveiby, 2001). To date, no study has addressed the role of strategic thinking and IB as convertible acts of external knowledge that guide strategic action. Most, if not all, external knowledge rests in four major pockets (Sveiby, 2001).

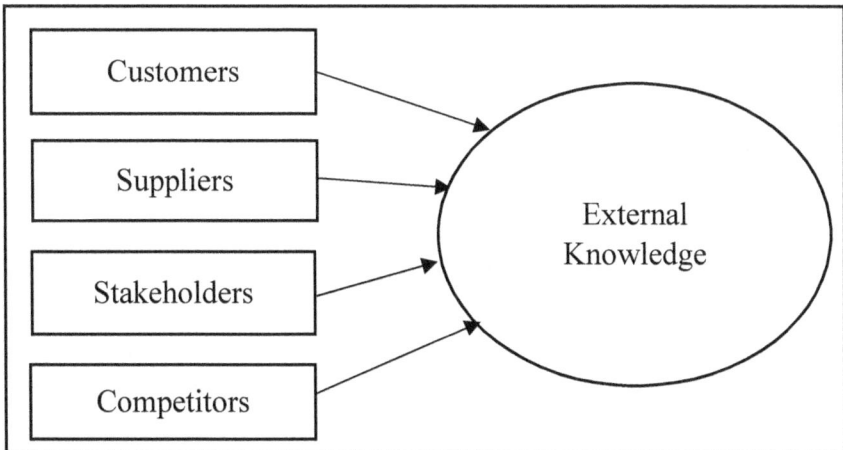

Figure 1. External pockets of derived market knowledge.

Figure 1 represents the pockets of external knowledge—pockets where knowledge is found, captured, and acquired by firm members and management. These pockets strengthen the links related to the knowledge-based view of the firm. Under this theory, the two types of knowledge are categorized as procedural and technological (Grant, 1996). Both knowledge types provide firms with tremendous strategic advantages (e.g., a higher level of predictability of landscape changes, tactical actions, market updates, and new technologies).

The resource-based view of the firm had its start in the early 1990s when much of the literature focused on the development of resources and the change of firm capabilities over time. Unlike the resource-based view of the firm, the knowledge-based view considers knowledge acquisition, transfer, and spillovers (Malmberg & Maskell, 2002) and knowledge integration across the firm's landscape (Eisenhardt & Santos, 2002). Eisenhardt and Santos (2002) maintained that the intangible and heterogeneous nature of "knowledge-based thinking is enormously important for understanding a number of central topics in strategy, including acquisitions, alliances, and strategic choice" (p. 2). Conversely, but not dissimilarly, the resource-based view purports that a firm's competitive advantage is based on its resources and capabilities—both tangible and intangible—that are valuable and inimitable (Barney et al., 2001).

Strategic Thinking

Strategic thinking has had many focal transmutations in its theoretical development. It started in the 1960s, focusing on strategic planning, moved to management in the 1970s, and is currently focused on strategic thinking (Norzailan, Yusof, & Othman, 2016)—cognitive-orientated aspects of strategy. Liedtka (1998) pointed out five salient competencies for strategic thinking capability: systems perspective, intent-focused, intelligent opportunism, thinking in time, and hypothesis-driven. These competencies are internally activated before and during strategic planning. To acquire these competencies, one must align one's knowledge base, habits, and thinking paradigm with real time, maneuver to capture critical striking opportunity, and assess potential problem analysis.

To this point, Hargadon (2002) asked, "Why is it so difficult for organizations to learn from their experiences and why it is so difficult for them to forget these lessons when forced with a changed environment" (p. 42). The strategic thinking mindset influences one's abilities, perceptions, and capabilities to create new opportunities but should not be viewed as thinking in isolation (Alsaaty, 2007). This mindset is not limited to upper-echelon decision-makers; rather, strategic thinking is a cognitive model that should permeate through all levels of the organization collaboratively, simultaneously, and expeditiously before Murphy's Law takes effect.

Strategic thinking is a critical element in strategizing. One possesses the knowledge, makes decisions within the firm based on competitive positioning, and creates sustainable advantages on an ongoing basis. Strategic thinking is a cognitive process (Calabrese & Costa, 2015; Mintzberg, 1978) that materializes through the multiple layers of the planning cycle and can be put into real-time action to drive employees' behaviors (Pandza, 2011) to reach strategic goals. In application, strategic thinkers logically use information (internal or external), select appropriate pieces of the information, reinterpret the information, make sense of the related and unrelated events of the situation, and link the information to internal challenges or opportunities that lead to major initiatives.

The objective of strategic thinkers is to see beyond the assumptions, examine the underpinnings of an issue or challenge, and seize opportunity (Pisapia, Pang, Hee, Lin, & Morris, 2009). With the objective of strategic thinking in mind, firms are not created equally in terms of resources and/or capabilities of employees and managers alike. That is why the ongoing acquisition of new knowledge and strategic direction in the minds of management can be antithetical to the old paradigm of firm strategy, where managers tenaciously cling to conventional strategy in the face of challenge and adversary.

Strategic thinking, sometimes referred to as unconventional thinking, has been positively linked to managers' ability to meet new and unforeseen challenges with greater effectiveness, rather than patterned responses to new and or unforeseen challenges (McKenzie, Woolf, van Winkelen, & Morgan, 2009). Ackoff (1999) surveyed managers who purported to situationally frame past experiences and context without cognitive flexibility (Spiro, Vispoel, Schmitz, Samarapungavan, & Boerger, 1987) when it came to issues and problems with incomplete or contradictory interpretations.

Given these points, McKenzie et al. (2009) purported that non-strategic thinkers typically pursue conventional responses in the face of challenge; the CEO respondents agreed they used conventional thinking by ignoring contradictory information, passing the problem along, seeking excessive clarity on issues, and making quick solutions by eliminating contradictory information. Moon (2013) collected data from the top and middle managers and front-line employees in 217 firms. Moon showed that strategic thinking was positively and significantly related to management's attitude toward risk-seeking behaviors but negatively related to the formalization of the decision-making process. Moon also showed that strategic thinking was positively related to increased profit, sales revenue, and the active pursuit of market share.

Strategic thinking positively correlated with executives' openness to experience, accumulated work experience, and cognitive ability, according to Dragoni, Oh, Vankatwyk, and Tesluck (2011) but negatively correlated with years of experience. In hierarchal regression results, after controlling for gender, ethnicity, years of experience, and time in a lead role, Dragoni et al. reported cognitive ability to be strongly related to strategic thinking. These findings are significant as they additionally highlight how the associated levels of responsibility held by managers aid their ability to think strategically.

Innovative Behavior

IB is known to increase performance and sustainability, engage employees' competitiveness, and propel organizational success (Amabile, 1988; Carmeli, Meitar, & Weisberg, 2006; Scott & Bruce, 1994). In a landmark study, Scott and Bruce (1994) viewed IB as an individual process because it is individuals who "develop, carry, react and modify ideas leading to action involving the actionable ideas" (p. 580). The construct of IB has two different definitions. Kleysen and Street (2001) defined IB to involve "all individual actions directed at the generation, introduction and or application of beneficial novelty at any organizational level" (p. 285). De Jong and Den Hartog (2007) defined IB as "directed towards the initiation and application of new and useful ideas, processes, products, or procedures" (p. 43).

IB is a driver that enhances many of the firm's growth, revenue, and product outcomes largely based on its four dimensions: idea exploration, idea generation, idea championing, and idea implementation (De Jong & Den Hartog, 2010; Scott & Bruce, 1994; West & Farr, 1989). Organizational management that receives external knowledge and assimilates it toward innovative ends is vital to employee IB and capabilities (Cohen & Levinthal, 1990). Stenholm (2011) examined the role of IB on firm growth intentions in entrepreneurial businesses. The data were analyzed with hierarchical regression analysis while size, age, and industry (Almus & Nerlinger, 1999; Cliff, 1998; Delmar & Wiklund, 2008; Stenholm, 2011) were controlled—a method consistent with others. Stenholm found that IB was associated with firm growth efforts as IB affects growth and has demands on internal capabilities needed to employ scarce resources to bring innovation to fruition. In the same vein, IB was positively linked with external work contacts and innovative employee output, based on a study that sampled 94 firms and 703 workers (De Jong & Den Hartog, 2008). Organizational climate and IB were positively related, based on data collected from 39 upper-level managers and 105 front-line managers. The analysis reported climate as significantly related to innovative behavior and having a strong relationship with EO (Kang, Matusik, Kim, & Phillips, 2016).

In a seminal study, Scott and Bruce (1994) examined the effects of IB on employee perceptions of the organizational climate fueled by innovation. Their model consisted of four levels of analysis: individual, leader, workgroup, and climate. In the underpinning of their multilayered model, Scott and Bruce purported that climate, employee psychological perception of appropriate behaviors, leadership support for innovation, manager expectations, and systematic problem solving were positively related to individual IB. With very few studies that have tested the manifest and latent effects of IB in business, Xerri and Brunetto (2011) focused on how knowledge transfer manifests within organizations and influences IB. The view of IB was such that it increases and grows stronger when knowledge is shared equitably between firm members. Xerri and Brunetto viewed these capabilities from the inside out by internalizing rewarding and supporting mechanisms provided to employees as cultural and structural apparatuses to cultivate IB. Social capital, trust, relational strength, and culture positively impacted employee IB.

Absorptive Capacity

There has been a tremendous number of foci in the literature on the use and implementation of knowledge using firm capabilities directed at the acquisition of new knowledge that accelerates intrafirm advances, expeditiously acquiring knowledge to propel the implementation of new knowledge and developing fast-track methodologies from conception to the production of products and services. However, sparse literature has provided insight into the moderating role of ACAP. There has been little theoretical rejuvenation of ACAP in terms of its relationship between IB and employee strategic thinking and its impact on organization-level EO and strategy. Stock et al. (2001) explained, "A potentially relevant construct that has received comparatively little attention with respect to product development is absorptive capacity" (p. 78).

ACAP is an interorganizational phenomenon that includes developing processes for new products, generating ideas, and exploiting them into products or services that will outperform competitors in the marketplace (Cohen & Levinthal, 1990; Jansen et al., 2005; Sciascia, D'oria, Bruni, & Larrañeta, 2014; Zahra & George, 2002), serve to increase firm-level problem-solving skills (Kim, 1998), and engage involuntary knowledge spillovers (Gulati, 1998). ACAP consists of four dimensions: acquisition, assimilation, transformation, and exploitation (Zahra & George, 2002). Newly acquired knowledge and employee performance due to high levels of ACAP are related to new product development. Cohen and Levinthal (1990) indicated that ACAP is associated with various levels of employee performance. The ease with which employees learn from external sources enhances internal capabilities—both realized and potential.

In line with Cohen and Levinthal (1990), Tsai (2001) proposed that organizational units can transfer knowledge across several units to increase innovation and organizational performance, taking an inside-out perspective. Tsai collected data from 24 businesses and 36 business units that showed a significant and positive effect on business unit invention and performance abilities. Tsai suggested that units with higher levels of ACAP are associated with higher levels of performance and innovation. The more work units transfer knowledge, the higher the success rates of assimilating the newly learned knowledge toward speed to market, the performance of business units, and commercialization of products (Tsai, 2001). Although the acquisition of external information is fundamental to learning and knowledge sharing between management and employees, transformation and exploitation is vital to this process and play the role of integrating existing knowledge and the newly acquired external information.

The transformational stage of the absorptive process serves to break down interfirm silos, producing gains in productivity and transmitting the entrepreneurial spirit. A potential disconnecting factor between the newly acquired information and internal capabilities could create a mismatch that disrupts the internal structural balance. Scaringella, Miles, and Truong (2017) maintained that management could find techniques to realign both innovation and new information when this internal balance is disrupted. Further, the exploitation of new information, enmeshed in the absorptive process, has a strong basis in firm-level EO. This phase is the culmination of efforts that lead to the commercialization of products and services.

Zahra and George (2002) argued that ACAP has unrealized and realized dimensions vital to intrafirm knowledge spillovers. These dimensions are dynamic capabilities that often are potential, but due to high costs of in-house research and development, much of knowledge sharing and learning has been virtually eliminated or unrealized; moreover, overall, what remains explicit in firm knowledge acquisition and assimilation to exploitation is that firms often need information that lies outside their core competence. Therefore, the underpinning of ACAP, the explication of its dimensions, is critical to understanding both realized and potential fusion of external knowledge because higher ACAP means increased outputs and performance.

Potential and Realized Absorptive Capacity

ACAP has been assigned various units of analysis such as countries, organizations, and intra-organizational divisions (Zahra & George, 2002). ACAP has been viewed through several theoretical lenses, including inward knowledge transfer, organizational learning, strategic management, innovation, and organizations as learning systems (Zahra & George, 2002) to name a few. These past lenses did not consider the effect employee behaviors might have on potential and realized capabilities and its relationship with employee entrepreneurial behaviors.

Cohen and Levinthal (1990) conceptually developed potential ACAP (PACAP) and realized ACAP (RACAP). They described the two dimensions of ACAP as encapsulating how managers internalize and acquire external information and how managers leverage useful information from the external landscape to commercialize realized products or services. Knowledge acquired externally is not altogether useful in and of itself but adds to the capital needed to infuse the institutional memory for future organizational development. Nevertheless, the mere fact that organizations are receptive to acquiring external knowledge is ideal for internal transformational processes related to the interfirm value-adding process linkages. Another aspect of these dimensions is that management values external knowledge because it adds to the human capital needed to assimilate and materialize the commercialization of outputs. Therefore, both realized and potential ACAP are not mutually exclusive as they are both performance enhancers and should be cultivated by structure and leadership.

ACAP's four dimensions are categorized as either *potential* or *realized*. Potential capabilities refer to the *acquisition* and *assimilation* of newly acquired external knowledge. Acquisition refers to how firms identify and acquire external knowledge that is particularly vital to its operations. Assimilation is the firm's routines and processes used to analyze, interpret, and reinterpret information. Realized ACAP consists of *transformation* and *exploitation*. Transformation refers to the refinement process once new external knowledge has been collected and identified. At this stage, the information is internally coded and converted to a body of knowledge in which the organization's ecosystem absorbs knowledge into the needed gaps located within the system. Exploitation is applying the knowledge and the process orientation embedded into the firm's structure to allow for refinement. The important elements of this dimension are the procedure, structure, processes, and realization of products and services and the ability to sustain these realized activities over time.

Entrepreneurial Orientation

Rauch, Wiklund, Lumpkin, and Frese (2009) defined *entrepreneurial orientation* as "the strategy-making processes that provide organizations with a basis for entrepreneurial decisions and actions" (p. 3). Stam and Elfring (2008) similarly yet alternatively defined EO as "the processes, structures, and behaviors of firms that are characterized by innovativeness, proactiveness, and risk taking"

(p. 98; see also Covin & Slevin, 1989; Miller, 1983). The domains of EO are innovativeness, proactiveness, and risk-taking (Rauch et al., 2009). Innovativeness refers to the ethos in which a firm cultivates, supports, and drives creative ideas that can result in new products, services, and processes; proactiveness refers to the alertness and awareness of future needs, opportunities, or issues that could serve to beat competitors to the market; and risk-taking involves management allocation of resources into ventures in the face of uncertainty (Brettel, Chomik, & Flatten, 2015; Miller, 1983; Rauch et al., 2009).

EO is best described as breaking away from existing routines (Kirzner, 1999); it disrupts existing structures and markets as a disequilibriating force (Schumpeter, 1950). However, Schumpeter (1950) attributed higher status to the behaviors of the entrepreneurially oriented and suggested that this type of firm-level ethos inoculates members with abilities that lead markets with capabilities not imitable by competitors; therefore, these entrepreneurially oriented firms that are proactive and take risk often have advantages that can creatively disrupt existing markets. Simply, EO comprises organizational processes, methods, practices, and decision-making methodologies not only at the individual level (Jelenc et al., 2015) but at the firm level of analysis (Lumpkin & Dess, 1996; Miller, 1983). EO might increase in intensity if influenced by innovative action provided the necessary faculties to commercialize new developments (Wales, Parida, & Patel, 2013), transfer knowledge (Chen & Huang, 2009; Tsai, 2001) to enhance learning capabilities to sustain competitive advantages, and harness employee IB.

The EO literature has purported that firms with high levels of EO experience higher levels of performance (Wang & Zang, 2005; Wiklund, 1999). Because of EO's vitality to performance, managers cultivate an ethos of EO at the firm level to drive strategy (Miller, 1983). EO is one of the most dynamic constructs in the business strategy literature (Brettel et al., 2015). The dynamism of EO is at the foundation of entrepreneurship and entrepreneurial strategy in that EO has been related to leaders' decision-making and aligned with strategy execution (Brettel et al., 2015), which is particularly important in the business context because many small and large businesses are in constant survival mode (Zahra, Sapienza, & Davidsson, 2006). However, Zahra et al. (2006) said scant literature has explained how business capabilities are created, cultivated, and implemented, considering the scarcity of resources and knowledge expertise. This lack of knowledge can hinder competitive positioning in hostile environments and pose serious threats to firm-level employee risk-taking, proactive propensity, and employee psychological risk (Covin & Slevin, 1989).

Leading managers seek to acquire new knowledge to expand their competitive advantage and secure strategic positioning in their respective markets. Wales et al. (2013) examined the moderating role of EO on ACAP related to entrepreneurial performance measures (i.e., sales growth, operating profit, and return-on-assets growth). Wales et al. suggested that EO highly influences financial returns, which justifies a strong preexisting relationship. However, the measures are dependent on the level of EO ethos within management. EO creates an opportunity to make process gains and could translate to financial returns based on firm-level EO.

Brown, Davidsson, and Wiklund (2001) and Shane (2000) expressed the need for future research to implement individual-level factors and variables that could be tested against different types of knowledge attainment strategies. Figure 2 presents the missing link between strategic thinking and IB individual factors on firm-level EO and the moderating role of ACAP as a determinate of the relationship strength among the variables of risk-taking, innovativeness, and proactiveness. Figure 2 shows how external knowledge enters through the firm at the individual level (e.g., management) and management deciphers the knowledge and transforms it with ACAP—realized and potential. This process moderates the strength of firm-level EO.

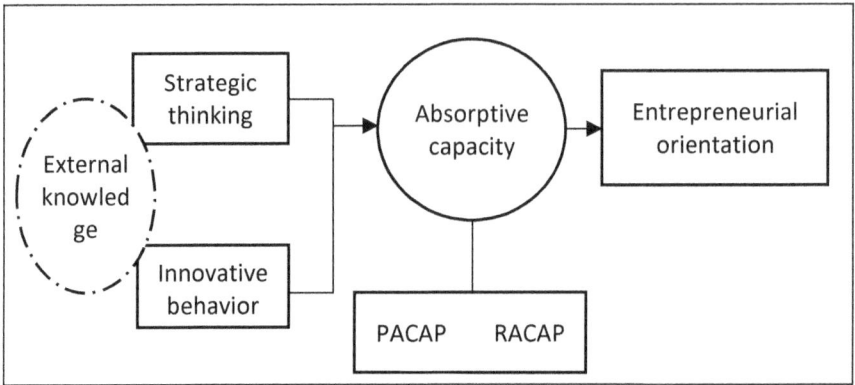

Figure 2. Moderating role of ACAP and strategic behaviors.

Managers' and employees' ability to analyze new knowledge from external sources, assimilate and transform the information, and exploit it commercially is the utility of ACAP. What is easily inferred from the theoretical model is that strategic thinking does have a significant influence on employee behaviors because, by its very nature, strategic-thinking managers can see beyond the basic assumptions and generalities of the firm's current market position; they can reframe issues from a systems perspective while using previous experiences to find new directions that will develop organically to compete on the business landscape simultaneously.

IB is the secondary variable in this model as newly acquired knowledge is approached with the intent to create novel ideas and move them to tangible innovation. This is a substantive aspect directly related to the strength of realized ACAP. IB is part of the organization's climate. Suppose there is a perceived view of IB for the sake of innovation. In that case, firm members are more apt to support the risk of others and be more willing to disregard the psychological risk of behaving innovatively themselves. A pro-innovative climate (Scott & Bruce, 1994) will positively affect both the risk and gains of employee IB and reduce IB inertia inherent to failed ideas in many business environments (Yuan & Woodman, 2010). This is why IB is included in Figure 2 as a pro-climate factor vital to the way external knowledge is inserted into potential and realized capabilities related to increasing EO.

ACAP, shown in the model as a moderating variable, influences the strength in the relationship between strategic thinking, IB, and EO. A high ACAP adds strength to the relationship with EO. Potential and realized ACAP play significant roles in influencing the strength of EO's innovativeness, risk-taking, and proactiveness dimensions without signs of diminishing returns over time (Scaringella et al., 2017).

Figure 2 agrees with statements made by Nickerson and Zenger (2004), who contended, "The state of a firm's knowledge can be advanced by either absorbing existing knowledge external to the firm or by developing new knowledge by first identifying a problem and then discovering a valuable new solution" (p. 2). Based on the theoretical model, the outcome factor is a higher EO and management's ethos at the firm level. This theoretical model presents three propositions for future research:

P1: Strategic thinking has a positive relationship with EO when moderated by ACAP.

P2: IB has a positive relationship with EO when moderated by ACAP.

P3: Strategic thinking and IB are positively related to EO.

DISCUSSION

The theoretical model and propositions assist practitioners and academics alike on the quest to better understand the moderating role of ACAP on strategic behaviors. This research also supports the strategic paradigm shift toward the strategic cognition of employees and managers—how they think strategically and how IB is applied to incoming knowledge, and how knowledge is internally transformed into realized capabilities. Additionally, the theoretical results align with Vera, Nemanich, Valez-Castrillon, and Werner (2016). External knowledge can help the firm develop a broader knowledge base, keep abreast of cutting-edge technologies, and prevent waste of resources and time-wasting activities. Higher levels of EO are not initiated on their own. However, they are magnified when strategic thinking and IB are woven into the transitionary process of knowledge fusion and transmutation of the knowledge at the firm level of analysis. The presented propositions can be tested either qualitatively or quantitatively to compare industry types, cultures, and small and large organizations.

CONCLUSION

This research began with a central question in mind: What is the moderating influence of ACAP among strategic thinking, IB, and EO? This central question was followed by secondary questions related to the role of strategic behaviors (i.e., strategic thinking, IB, and EO) and their place in the knowledge-based view theory. The presented propositions provide new approaches and theoretical linkage concerning ACAP and its moderating relationship between strategic thinking, IB, and EO. The model in Figure 2 adds to the integral role of strategic behaviors' unexamined relationship to entrepreneurial behaviors.

Based on the theoretical analysis and the assessment of current literature, before EO can be actualized and realized, external knowledge should first be viewed in terms of firm members' capabilities required to transform and commercialize ideas to final products or services. The theoretical linkages and propositions presented here between knowledge and final product and service development are central to the work of Guerras-Martín, Madhok, and Montoro-Sánchez (2014) who analyzed employee behaviors through strategy making and strategic directions. Although Guerras-Martín et al. were concerned primarily with the resource-based view of the firm, this theoretical development focuses on the firm's knowledge base and the inclusion of constructs based on how knowledge is transmitted externally and the behaviors of employees to transmute the knowledge to increase EO internally.

In this research, EO is the explanatory variable in terms of its position in the view of the firm paradigm. There is a substantial number of indicators to purport a relationship between IB and EO (Gross, 2016a), but a lack of discussion or empirical evidence of the theoretical links between strategic thinking and IB, and their inclusion in the knowledge base of the firm and the potential effects of a moderating relationship on EO. Madhok and Marques (2014) raised concerns regarding a contemporary view of strategic management and how strategy ought to be viewed insofar as the dynamic changes in today's business landscapes.

REFERENCES

Ackoff, R. L. (1999). *Ackoff's best: His classic writings on management*. New York, NY: John Wiley & Sons.

Allee, V. (2000). Knowledge networks and communities of practice. *OD Practitioner, 32*(4), 4-13.

Almus, M., & Nerlinger, E. A. (1999). Growth of new technology-based firms: Which factors matter? *Small Business Economics, 13*(2), 141-154.

Alsaaty, F. M. (2007). Entrepreneurs: Strategic thinkers in search of opportunities. *Journal of Business & Economics Research, 5*(2).

Amabile, T. M. (1988). A model of creativity and innovation in organizations. *Research in Organizational Behavior, 10*(1), 123-167.

Barney, J., Wright, M., & Ketchen, D. J., Jr. (2001). The resource-based view of the firm: Ten years after 1991. *Journal of Management, 27*(6), 625-641.

Birdi, K., Leach, D., & Magadley, W. (2016). The relationship of individual capabilities and environmental support with different facets of designers' innovative behavior. *Journal of Product Innovation Management, 33*(1), 19-35.

Brettel, M., Chomik, C., & Flatten, T. C. (2015). How organizational culture influences innovativeness, proactiveness, and risk-taking: Fostering entrepreneurial orientation in SMEs. *Journal of Small Business Management, 53*(4), 868-885.

Brown, T. E., Davidsson, P., & Wiklund, J. (2001). An operationalization of Stevenson's conceptualization of entrepreneurship as opportunity-based firm behavior. *Strategic Management Journal, 22*(10), 953-968.

Burns, D. J. (1987). *The effects of uniqueness seeking and sensation seeking upon innovative behavior and the adoption process* (Doctoral dissertation, Kent State University). Retrieved from https://pfeifferuniversity-on-worldcat-org.pfeiffer.idm.oclc.org/search?queryString=no:935810303 &databaseList=283

Burns, D. J. (2007). Toward an explanatory model of innovative behavior. *Journal of Business and Psychology, 21*(4), 461-488.

Calabrese, A., & Costa, R. (2015). Strategic thinking and business innovation: Abduction as cognitive element of leaders' strategizing. *Journal of Engineering and Technology Management, 38*, 24-36.

Calantone, R. J., Schmidt, J. B., & Di Benedetto, C. A. (1997). New product activities and performance: The moderating role of environmental hostility. *Journal of Product Innovation Management, 14*(3), 179-189.

Carmeli, A., Meitar, R., & Weisberg, J. (2006). Self-leadership skills and innovative behavior at work. *International Journal of Manpower, 27*(1), 75-90.

Cassiman, B., & Veugelers, R. (2006). In search of complementarity in innovation strategy: Internal R&D and external knowledge acquisition. *Management Science, 52*(1), 68-82.

Chen, C. J., & Huang, J. W. (2009). Strategic human resource practices and innovation performance—The mediating role of knowledge management capacity. *Journal of Business Research, 62*(1), 104-114.

Cliff, J. E. (1998). Does one size fit all? Exploring the relationship between attitudes towards growth, gender, and business size. *Journal of Business Venturing, 13*(6), 523-542.

Cohen, W. M., & Levinthal, D. A. (1990). Absorptive capacity: A new perspective on learning and innovation. *Administrative Science Quarterly*, 128-152.

Covin, J. G., & Slevin, D. P. (1989). Strategic management of small firms in hostile and benign environments. *Strategic Management Journal, 10*(1), 75-87.

De Jong, J. P., & Den Hartog, D. N. (2007). How leaders influence employees' innovative behaviour. *European Journal of Innovation Management, 10*(1), 41-64.

De Jong, J. P., & Den Hartog, D. N. (2008). Innovative work behavior: Measurement and validation. *EIM Business and Policy Research*, 1-27.

De Jong, J. P., & Den Hartog, D. N. (2010). Measuring innovative work behaviour. *Creativity and Innovation Management, 19*(1), 23-36.

Delmar, F., & Wiklund, J. (2008). The effect of small business managers' growth motivation on firm growth: A longitudinal study. *Entrepreneurship Theory and Practice, 32*(3), 437-457.

Dragoni, L., Oh, I. S., Vankatwyk, P., & Tesluk, P. E. (2011). Developing executive leaders: The relative contribution of cognitive ability, personality, and the accumulation of work experience in predicting strategic thinking competency. *Personnel Psychology, 64*(4), 829-864.

Droge, C., & Calantone, R. (1996). New product strategy, structure, and performance in two environments. *Industrial Marketing Management, 25*(6), 555-566.

Easterby-Smith, M., Graça, M., Antonacopoulou, E., & Ferdinand, J. (2008). Absorptive capacity: A process perspective. *Management Learning, 39*(5), 483-501.

Ebben, J. J., & Johnson, A. C. (2005). Efficiency, flexibility, or both? Evidence linking strategy to performance in small firms. *Strategic Management Journal, 26*(13), 1249-1259.

Eisenhardt, K., & Santos, F. (2000). Knowledge-based view: A new theory of strategy? In A. Pettigrew, H. Thomas, & R. Whittington (Eds.), *Handbook of strategy and management* (pp. 31-47). Thousand Oaks, CA: Sage.

Galunic, D. C., & Rodan, S. (1998). Research notes and communications: Resource recombinations in the firm:

Knowledge structures and the potential for Schumpeterian innovation. *Strategic Management Journal*, *19*(12), 1193-1201.

Grant, R. M. (1996). Toward a knowledge-based theory of the firm. *Strategic Management Journal*, *17*(S2), 109-122.

Gross, R. (2016a). *The impact of leadership styles on employee entrepreneurial orientation and innovative behavior: A comparative Analysis of American and Indian immigrant entrepreneurs* (Doctoral dissertation, Regent University). Retrieved from http://search.proquest.com/openview/ded1f395860c0208ebfc faceaebedf6d/1?pq-origsite=gscholar&cbl=18750&diss=y

Gross, R. (2016b). Towards an understanding of the relationship between leadership styles and strategic thinking: A small and medium enterprise perspective. *Journal of Business Studies Quarterly*, *8*(2), 22-39.

Gross, R., & Cabanda, E. (2016). Modelling the relationship between leadership styles and innovative behavior and entrepreneurial orientation in American firms. *Review of Business and Technology Research*, *13*(1),1-7.

Guerras-Martín, L. Á., Madhok, A., & Montoro-Sánchez, Á. (2014). The evolution of strategic management research: Recent trends and current directions. *BRQ Business Research Quarterly*, *17*(2), 69-76.

Gulati, R. (1998). Alliances and networks. *Strategic Management Journal*, *19*(4), 293-317.

Hargadon, A. B. (2002). Brokering knowledge: Linking learning and innovation. *Research in Organizational Behavior*, *24*, 41-85.

Hughes, B., & Wareham, J. (2010). Knowledge arbitrage in global pharma: A synthetic view of absorptive capacity and open innovation. *R&D Management*, *40*(3), 324-343.

Jansen, J. J., Van Den Bosch, F. A., & Volberda, H. W. (2005). Managing potential and realized absorptive capacity: How do organizational antecedents matter? *Academy of Management Journal*, *48*(6), 999-1015.

Jelenc, L., & Pisapia, J. (2015). Individual entrepreneurial behavior in Croatian IT firms: The contribution of strategic thinking skills. *Journal of Information and Organizational Sciences, 39*(2), 163-182.

Jelenc, L., Pisapia, J., & Ivanusic, N. (2015). Demographic variables influencing individual entrepreneurial orientation and strategic thinking capability. *Proceedings of the 10th international Scientific Conference on Economic and Social Development.* Retrieved from https://ssrn.com/abstract=2715121

Kang, J. H., Matusik, J. G., Kim, T. Y., & Phillips, J. M. (2016). Interactive effects of multiple organizational climates on employee innovative behavior in entrepreneurial firms: A cross-level investigation. *Journal of Business Venturing, 31*(6), 628-642.

Kim, L. (1998). Crisis construction and organizational learning: Capability building in catching-up at Hyundai Motor. *Organization Science, 9*(4), 506-521.

Kirzner, I. M. (1999). Creativity and/or alertness: A reconsideration of the Schumpeterian entrepreneur. *The Review of Austrian Economics, 11*(1-2), 5-17.

Kleysen, R. F., & Street, C. T. (2001). Toward a multi-dimensional measure of individual innovative behavior. *Journal of intellectual Capital, 2*(3), 284-296.

Liedtka, J. M. (1998). Strategic thinking: Can it be taught? *Long Range Planning, 31*(1), 120-129.

Lumpkin, G. T., & Dess, G. G. (1996). Clarifying the entrepreneurial orientation construct and linking it to performance. *Academy of Management Review, 21*(1), 135-172.

Madhok, A., & Marques, R. (2014). Towards an action-based perspective on firm competitiveness. *BRQ Business Research Quarterly, 17*(2), 77-81.

Malmberg, A., & Maskell, P. (2002). The elusive concept of localization economies: Towards a knowledge-based theory of spatial clustering. *Environment and Planning A, 34*(3), 429-449.

McKenzie, J., Woolf, N., Van Winkelen, C., & Morgan, C. (2009). Cognition in strategic decision making: A model of non-conventional thinking capacities for complex situations. *Management Decision, 47*(2), 209-232.

Miller, D. (1983). The correlates of entrepreneurship in three types of firms. *Management Science, 29*(7), 770-791.

Mintzberg, H. (1978). Patterns in strategy formation. *Management Science, 24*(9), 934-948.

Moon, B. J. (2013). Antecedents and outcomes of strategic thinking. *Journal of Business Research, 66*(10), 1698-1708.

Nonaka, I., & Takeuchi, H. (1995). *The knowledge-creating company: How Japanese companies create the dynamics of innovation.* New York, NY: Oxford University Press.

Nickerson, J. A., & Zenger, T. R. (2004). A knowledge-based theory of the firm—The problem-solving perspective. *Organization Science, 15*(6), 617-632.

Norzailan, Z., Yusof, S. M., & Othman, R. (2016). Developing strategic leadership competencies. *Journal of Advanced Management Science, 4*(1), 66-71.

Pandza, K. (2011). Why and how will a group act autonomously to make an impact on the development of organizational capabilities? *Journal of Management Studies, 48*(5), 1015-1043.

Pisapia, J., Pang, N. S. K., Hee, T. F., Lin, Y., & Morris, J. D. (2009). A comparison of the use of strategic thinking skills of aspiring school leaders in Hong Kong, Malaysia, Shanghai, and the United States: An exploratory study. *International Education Studies, 2*(2), 46.

Rauch, A., Wiklund, J., Lumpkin, G. T., & Frese, M. (2009). Entrepreneurial orientation and business performance: An assessment of past research and suggestions for the future. *Entrepreneurship Theory and Practice, 33*(3), 761-787.

Roehrich, G. (2004). Consumer innovativeness: Concepts and measurements. *Journal of Business Research, 57*(6), 671-677.

Scaringella, L., Miles, R. E., & Truong, Y. (2017). Customers involvement and firm absorptive capacity in radical innovation: The case of technological spin-offs. *Technological Forecasting and Social Change.* Retrieved from https://www.researchgate.net/publication/312355628_Custo mers_involvement_and_firm_absorptive_capacity_in_radical _innovation_The_case_of_technological_spin-offs

Schumpeter, J. (1950). The process of creative destruction. In J. Schumpeter (Ed.), *Capitalism, socialism and democracy* (3rd ed., pp. 131-145). London, England: Allen and Unwin.

Sciascia, S., D'oria, L., Bruni, M., & Larrañeta, B. (2014). Entrepreneurial orientation in low-and medium-tech industries: The need for absorptive capacity to increase performance. *European Management Journal, 32*(5), 761-769.

Scott, S. G., & Bruce, R. A. (1994). Determinants of innovative behavior: A path model of individual innovation in the workplace. *Academy of Management Journal, 37*(3), 580-607.

Shane, S. (2000). Prior knowledge and the discovery of entrepreneurial opportunities. *Organization Science, 11*(4), 448-469.

Spiro, R. J., Vispoel, W. P., Schmitz, J. G., Samarapungavan, A., & Boerger, A. E. (1987). Knowledge acquisition for application: Cognitive flexibility and transfer in complex content domains. In B. K. Britton & S. M. Glynn (Eds.), *Executive control processes in reading* (pp. 177-199). Hillsdale, NJ: Lawrence Erlbaum.

Stam, W., & Elfring, T. (2008). Entrepreneurial orientation and new venture performance: The moderating role of intra-and extraindustry social capital. *Academy of Management Journal, 51*(1), 97-111.

Stenholm, P. (2011). Innovative behavior as a moderator of growth intentions. *Journal of Small Business Management*, *49*(2), 233-251.

Stock, G. N., Greis, N. P., & Fischer, W. A. (2001). Absorptive capacity and new product development. *The Journal of High Technology Management Research*, *12*(1), 77-91.

Sveiby, K. E. (2001). A knowledge-based theory of the firm to guide in strategy formulation. *Journal of Intellectual Capital*, *2*(4), 344-358.

Tsai, W. (2001). Knowledge transfer in intraorganizational networks: Effects of network position and absorptive capacity on business unit innovation and performance. *Academy of Management Journal*, *44*(5), 996-1004.

Vega-Jurado, J., Gutiérrez-Gracia, A., & Fernández-de-Lucio, I. (2009). Does external knowledge sourcing matter for innovation? Evidence from the Spanish manufacturing industry. *Industrial and Corporate Change*, *18*(4), 637-670.

Vera, D., Nemanich, L., Velez-Castrillon, S., & Werner, S. (2016). Knowledge-based and contextual factors associated with R&D teams' improvisation capability. *Journal of Management*, *42*(7), 1874-1903.

Wales, W. J., Parida, V., & Patel, P. C. (2013). Too much of a good thing? Absorptive capacity, firm performance, and the moderating role of entrepreneurial orientation. *Strategic Management Journal*, *34*(5), 622-633.

Wang, Z., & Zang, Z. (2005). Strategic human resources, innovation and entrepreneurship fit: A cross-regional comparative model. *International Journal of Manpower*, *26*(6), 544-559.

West, M. A., & Farr, J. L. (1989). Innovation at work: Psychological perspectives. *Social Behaviour*, *4*(1), 15-30.

Wiklund, J. (1999). The sustainability of the entrepreneurial orientation—Performance relationship. *Entrepreneurship: Theory and Practice*, *24*(1), 37-37.

Xerri, M., & Brunetto, Y. (2011). Fostering the Innovative behavior of SME employees: A social capital perspective.

Research & Practice in Human Resource Management, *19*(2), 1.

Yuan, F., & Woodman, R. W. (2010). Innovative behavior in the workplace: The role of performance and image outcome expectations. *Academy of Management Journal, 53*(2), 323-342.

Zahra, S. A., & George, G. (2002). Absorptive capacity: A review, reconceptualization, and extension. *Academy of Management Review, 27*(2), 185-203.

Zahra, S. A., Sapienza, H. J., & Davidsson, P. (2006). Entrepreneurship and dynamic capabilities: A review, model and research agenda. *Journal of Management Studies, 43*(4), 917-955.

Chapter 6:
Absorptive Capacity and Strategic Flexibility

Entrepreneurial business strategy-making must be the top priority of discussion in the business and entrepreneurial literature. Strategy-making in a general sense has been axiomatically viewed from a perspective of planning, whereby an unplanned strategy is deemed to be causative enough of the successes or failures of a firm's strategy and performance outcomes. Simply, there is a lack of studies explicating the effects of slack resources and absorptive capacity (ACAP) on business-level strategy transitions.

This chapter approaches business strategy from a resource-based view of the firm (Barney, 1986; Feurer & Chaharbaghi, 1994; Robins & Wiersema, 1995) using the theoretical basis of strategic flexibility, which suggests that when business firms are flexible with internal resources (i.e., assets, human capital, information, knowledge, and technology), they are better able to create dynamic strategies that allow tactical changes in the firm's environmental position and adaptiveness (Matthyssens, Pauwels, & Vandenbempt, 2005; Srour, Baird, & Schoch, 2016; Zhou & Wu, 2010). This study provides three propositions for future research to confirm the impact of slack resources and ACAP on firm strategy flexibility in tumultuous business landscapes.

INTRODUCTION

Miles and Snow (1978) provided four generic, adaptive strategies that firms can *choose* based on external and internal constraints. However, in addition to understanding this taxonomy, proposed is the notion that to adapt a generic strategy, a firm's slack resources and ACAP are guiding mechanisms; this is often missing as a proponent of strategic flexibility in extant literature. Also neglected in the literature is the role that ACAP plays when it is internally intensified as to acquiring external knowledge, assimilating it, and transforming it internally.

Marlin and Geiger (2015) maintained, "There is scant research on slack and organizational outcomes utilizing firms outside of the manufacturing industry" (p. 2340). In many regards, there tends to be a parochial view of business strategy-making; this view does not reflect the true nature of strategy-making for businesses that operate in tumultuous environments with high uncertainty; instead, strategy decisions in this context should be viewed as complex, erratic, and dynamic (Ensign, 2008).

Based on this view, a proposition is purported: business-level strategy might be influenced largely by slack resource deployment as a response to push–pull environmental dynamics rather than by entrepreneurs' personal philosophy or choice. Although entrepreneurs make informed strategy decisions, their decisions may not align with their internal resources and capabilities due to environmental uncertainty and resource scarcity. Entrepreneurs' deployment of slack resources and intensity of ACAP can be identified as mechanisms to attain a generic strategy (e.g., prospector, defender, analyzer, or reactor).

From this perspective and reinterpretation of Miles and Snow's (1978) taxonomy, entrepreneurs do not choose a strategy *per se* because the firm, in many cases, operates at the impulse of environmental complexities. Environmental forces and internal resource deployment play major roles in strategic trajectory—neither are mutually exclusive. Optimistically, when internal slack resources are applied toward a new project (e.g., new product development or addition to a core service) and if ACBP is intensified, the business sets out on a strategic trajectory; the deployment of internal resources acts as an environmental response in either a *prospecting* or *defensive* strategy.

Most, if not all, of the strategic literature, have focused more on "the relations between organizational environment, strategic process, strategic content, organizational performances, and many other variables" (Alfirević, Pavičić, & Gnjidić, 2014, p. 93) and less on absorbed or unabsorbed slack resources to bolster tactics during strategy transition. Therefore, the current research proposes that entrepreneurial firms merely transition between Miles and Snow's (1978) generic strategies based on the deployment of organizational slack resources and intensity of ACAP. The entrepreneurship business landscape is dynamic and tumultuous. Entrepreneurs need to be increasingly adaptive to environment and industry changes compared with their larger counterparts. Adapting to the environment can be a slow process for an entrepreneurial firm, or entrepreneurs can remain insular from the larger network, losing out on potential external knowledge. Contrarily, if external networks are cultivated, and social capital is accrued, knowledge can then be dispersed among interdependencies (e.g., suppliers, customers, partners, and technology). The interdependent relationship is oriented around the absorption of knowledge.

This knowledge might be related to the use of technology, innovation, or just simple network collaboration. Business strategy must remain flexible and adaptable regarding push-pull environment demands due to the increasingly complex business landscape (Raymond & Bergeron, 2008) and uncertainty of the future, and technological capabilities in the larger network of interdependencies (Desarbo, Benedetto, Song, & Sinha, 2005).

The current research adds to theory by developing propositions to extend business strategy with an *inward* view and guided by the resource-based view (Barney, 1991) for further research and development. The resource-based view sees resources as rare, imitable, and valuable (Nyberg, Reilly, Essman, & Rodrigues, 2017). Exploring literature on this elicits a clearer understanding of the influence of ACAP and slack on strategic business advancement (Gimenez, 2000). Guided by this perspective, it is important to note that Miles and Snow's (1978) taxonomy was originally intended for corporate organizations (Desbarbo et al., 2005) but can and ought to be applied to business strategy. Business environment engagement adds to the competitiveness of the economy as small- and medium-sized enterprises (SMEs) are forerunners of innovation. Based on that assumption, "there is limited evidence regarding the role of organizational slack on SME innovation adoption" (Franquesa & Brandyberry, 2009 p. 26). Franquesa and Brandyberry (2009) confirmed, "The role of organizational slack in the context of small firms represents an important gap in our understanding of slack-innovation relationships" (p. 26). The antecedents of business strategy based on the taxonomy developed by Miles and Snow is nonexistent in extant literature. Therefore, the current research explores and uncovers theoretical gaps between business strategic adaptiveness influenced by ACAP and the deployment of slack resources.

LITERATURE REVIEW

Entrepreneurs intuitively deploy strategies to fit their landscape—to compete with other firms in their industry—and conduct extensive environmental scanning of related and, at times, unrelated business strategies to acquire new knowledge that has not previously existed inside the firm. However, there is a chasm between a firm's internal slack resource usage and ACAP influence on business strategy. According to Miles and Snow's (1978) taxonomy, there are four strategy types: *prospectors, analyzers, reactors,* and *defenders.* These strategies are adaptive (Miles, Snow, Meyer, & Coleman, 1978). Yet, the theory does not acknowledge the influence of environment changes as in the value chain, regulations, scarcity, and the probability of adapting and readapting to environments through critical allocation to new or existing projects that require the deployment of slack resources. Entrepreneurs' view of slack can be either constraining or unconstraining. For example, an owner might be encouraged with slack resources and use them to spur innovation. In contrast, management might increase ACAP, using new knowledge as a mechanism to connect capabilities with realized potential and assimilate and commercialize resources toward environment opportunities (Gross, 2016a).

Investigating these multidimensional constructs facilitates not only a theoretical understanding of their influence on business strategy but it is needed to fill the gap (Ensign, 2008; Pettigrew, 1992) among scholars' varying views of business strategy and the utility of slack resources and intensity of ACAP to adapt a strategy to internal and environment activity. Entrepreneurs pursue strategies based on inter- and intra-industry competitive forces coupled with their personal views and philosophies, past experiences, and a keen sense of the competition (Kotey & Meredith, 1997). Competition in a complex and unstable environment is a constant variable; entrepreneurs ought to analyze competitors' methods and adapt them to their strategic transition process. The question is not will we be first movers (i.e., by introducing new products; Kerin, Varadarajan, & Peterson, 1992) but rather *how* (Porter, 1980) will internal resources be used to follow a generic strategy transition from the reactor to an analyzer?

Strategy is dynamic (Ensign, 2008), and decision-making has unintended consequences (Mintzberg, 1994), which is why strategy can be emergent. But this emergent outlook calls for entrepreneurs to be adaptable to environmental needs and internal problems (i.e., administrative, entrepreneurial, or engineering). The emergent nature of strategy does not operate in isolation of the main strategy (i.e., entrepreneurs have preexisting tactics linked to various other decisions made at other points in time-related to other business areas).

At times, emergent strategies are more successful than strategies intended or planned without realized potential negative consequences (Mintzberg & McHugh, 1985). Ensign (2008) placed small entrepreneurial business strategies into three categories: *vertical dominance*, *dynamic dominance*, or *horizontal dominance*.

Vertical dominance describes the extent to which a manager's strategic decision cuts across other decisions set forth by firm members. Vertical dominance decisions are purposes ideas related to which industry to enter or if reengineering the existing structure could have a greater influence on the strategic choice (Burgelman, 2005; Ensign, 2008).

Dynamic dominance realizes changes to the environment and combines strategy with previously made choices. Dynamic dominance decisions induce major ripple effects across and within all levels of the firm, and strategic decisions made by entrepreneurs begin to converge on a leading strategic decision. Finally, strategic choices should include horizontal dominance, which has a profit-seeking motive and is combined with value goals. Each dominance factor must be embedded in strategy decisions and formulations if the strategy is viable and adaptive.

Chandler (1962) and Raymond and Bergeron (2008) expressed that scholars have disagreed about the malleability of a set plan comprising numerous tactics within a strategy while simultaneously pursuing multiple strategies from other areas of the business. The inability of entrepreneurs to blend, morph, or diversify strategic tactics intended to create new or unforeseen strategic combinations that have the potential to adapt to environmental demands but go unrealized is a constrained view of strategy. On the other end of the spectrum, scholars have purported that strategy should be fluid, changing, and malleable, where strategic thinking is the rule and not the exception—an unconstrained view of strategy (Gross, 2016b). This assertion is apparent in other cases where entrepreneurs accumulate, allocate, and maintain levels of slack resources to be used later as a safety net to meet unforeseen or future business objectives (Wefald, Katz, Downey, & Rust, 2010). Miles and Snow's (1978) taxonomy consists of four generic strategies dichotomized by a firm's ability, trajectory, and adaptability to environment pressures. As Miles and Snow identified them, the three conditions—or problems—are *entrepreneurial, engineering,* or *administrative.*

These conditions impose business constraints and are transitional and shifting, depending on the internal tactics and human capital aimed toward and applied to projects to enhance entrepreneurial constraints or detract from administrative problems to assist in reengineering the business structure. Contrarily, if unaddressed, constraints hinder a firm's ability to move toward a prospector's frontier; therefore, unaddressed constraints decrease the entrepreneurial spirit. Instead, there is a focus on administrative problems, which requires a defensive strategy. By focusing on an administrative solution, the firm will continue its existence at the least. An entrepreneurial solution is the commitment of resources to modify and change procedures and processes as a guide to proceed into a frontier. An engineering solution is answered when coordination and controls are implemented to help with unforeseen internal constraints. To find solutions to these problems, entrepreneurs need to apply slack resources to flex tactics that could swing the transition from one generic strategy to another and find those solutions with resources and knowledge to address problems that inhibit competitiveness and profitability.

The current research does not attempt to delineate generic strategies based on the intended consequential results from strategic constraints. This study does not provide comparisons between one strategy option versus another, although strategy choice and implementation are vital to business performance (Alfirević et al., 2014; Desarbo et al., 2005). However, what is proposed and presented is that when entrepreneurs adopt a strategy to eliminate or circumvent problem constraints, it poses challenges and requires internal change orientation and the use of slack. It also presents paradigm shifts—entrepreneurs must view slack resources not just as project-based work for management and employees but as mechanisms that steer a strategic position.

In the tumultuous business landscapes in which many entrepreneurs operate, change is inevitable. Entrepreneurs face challenges from external environmental factors and the internal allocation of slack resources and use thereof. Entrepreneurs' decisions regarding a strategic transition reflect a firm's view (e.g., resource-based view) and the vitality and value they hold for strategic thinking. In many cases, the problem facing entrepreneurs (i.e., entrepreneurial, engineering, or administrative) in terms of strategic constraints is the effect of consequential knowledge on their strategic transition as new developments in the environment take shape. Entrepreneurs employ many strategies with different objectives simultaneously, even as the dominant strategy matures over time (Hart, 1992; Mintzberg & Westley, 1992; Verreynne & Meyer, 2010). Therefore, strategy is not a predetermined path; perhaps it is dictated by environmental demands. Entrepreneurs can deploy slack resources to meet environmental demands and intensify the use of knowledge to adopt a strategy—as either a prospector, defender, analyzer, or reactor.

The daily operations of entrepreneurs are fraught with environmental constraints that larger organizations do not so much encounter. Some of this relates to the use of and fit of human capital, the supply chain, resources for continuous innovation, and acquisition of knowledge (Verreynne & Meyer, 2010). Entrepreneurs employ unique approaches to find solutions to strategy—the same as larger businesses; however, some businesses have smaller margins of error when pursing strategy based on resources (i.e., human and financial) and lack the ability to take on high-risk activities (Ahluwalia, Mahto, & Walsh, 2017), which gives rise to the application of the strategic taxonomy outlined by Miles and Snow (1978). The taxonomy's adaptive nature is better suited to analyze entrepreneurial firms' adaptiveness and environment activity (Gimenez, 2000; Olson & Currie, 1992).

The model provides an integrated view of the changing and tumultuous nature of the business firm's environment, emphasizing external and internal complexities. Most research on strategy has tended to focus on the end product of strategy—performance and entrepreneurs' capabilities, skills, and characteristics (Ingram, Kraśnicka, Wronka-Pośpiech, Głód, & Głód, 2016)—with minute focus on determinates or antecedents resulting from internally derived resources aligned to emerging tactics within a flexible strategic framework. The current examination goes a bit deeper. It provides strong antecedents of entrepreneurs' strategy adaptiveness and transitional movements along a strategic continuum with a notion that when slack resources are deployed and new knowledge is acquired, it contributes to entrepreneurs' tactical movements toward either a defending or a prospecting strategy—strategic flexibility. In the current purview, strategy is used to maneuver and mobilize resources and people around constraints to capture opportunities during times of certainty and uncertainty.

Desarbo et al. (2005) and Hambick (1983) suggested that the Miles and Snow (1978) model provides an incomplete view of strategy-making and positioning because it ignores contextual factors connected with the mobilization of internal resources. If it is to be used as a viable model, then a deeper analysis is needed. In this regard, Ingram et al. (2016) provided a dispassionate analysis consisting of two contextual factors (i.e., size of firm and age of the firm) and purported robust findings from the business literature. Ingram et al.'s results align with the conceptualization of the Miles and Snow model, whereby it was deemed applicable for future studies related to business strategy-making, developing, and executing processes.

The current research makes several attempts to add new interpretations to Miles and Snow's (1978) existing taxonomy and business theory with the central notion that not only do environment forces drive generic strategy transition, but the strategy is a result of the use of or lack of organizational slack resources and the intensity or inactivity of the acquisition and transformation of new knowledge. Also provided are theoretical models depicting organizational slack resources and ACAP interacting with the strategic transition. This contribution is unique because there has been a conflict of contexts in the literature regarding the vitality and contribution that new knowledge has on the effective use of slack on firm's businesses' adaptive tactics and strategies to meet environmental demands and internal constraints. These tasks are fulfilled by providing a literature review, followed by a conceptual framework with models, and suggestions for further research.

Miles and Snow's (1978) landmark study is tremendously influential in the strategy literature (Fiss, 2011; O'Regan & Ghobadian, 2004; Raymond & Bergeron, 2008; Tang & Zang, 2012); their model is a taxonomy that comprises four generic strategies. The taxonomy can be and is most often viewed as a process, adaptiveness of businesses to the pressures of constraints (Parnell, 2002), environment changes, and competition and provides entrepreneurs with three levels of problems—administrative, entrepreneurial, and engineering. The Miles and Snow model heavily emphasizes firms' adaptive behavior within an industry and environment as it is a business-level strategy. By and large, Miles and Snow's taxonomy provides theorists with a strong basis on which to examine adaptive strategies. However, the exploration has been sparse (Fiss, 2011). Fiss (2011) agreed with Zahra and Pearce (1990), who maintained, "There has been essentially no research on how firms of different strategic types utilize different organizational structures and coordination mechanisms" (p. 400). This falls in line with the attempts of the current study—to develop a strategy for an entrepreneurial firm as an emerging process and the use of internal resources employed to transition between strategies based on environment push–pull demands.

Miles and Snow's (1978) taxonomy has four strategy types: *defenders, prospectors, analyzers,* and *reactors.* According to Miles and Snow, the *defender* focuses on control and finding solutions to existing procedures, products, and problems. The focus is on niche offerings without considering outside domains for new environment opportunities (Gimenez, 2000; McDaniel & Kolari, 1987; Miles et al., 1978; Parnell, 2002; Shortell & Zajac, 1990). The defender maintains a position within a safe and secure product/service offering with greater emphasis on efficiency. This focus tends to remain narrow despite the advances of the competition, which in most cases would signal future maneuvering is needed. Rather, in this strategy type, entrepreneurs gridlock the business in a retreat position with little regard for learning from competitors and seeking new information beyond their boundaries. The view of the defender type is constrained—the management of these firms tends to control frontier activities and new knowledge flow from a centralized and historically based perspective (Ingram et al., 2016) with little regard for future opportunities and outlook.

The *prospector* is at the front of the strategy choice spectrum due to its association with innovation and innovative processes when combined to create new and novel products and service offerings (Ingram et al., 2016; Miles & Snow, 1978, 1986; Parnell, 2002). Prospectors are pioneers who prefer being the leader of environment changes. This strategy type embodies the spirit of emergence. In a constant state of external environmental scanning, prospectors maintain a healthy entrepreneurial spirit where change is not only welcomed but sought and reinforces management devotion to higher levels of strategic thinking (Gross, 2016a). Under this type, an owner's view is unconstrained—the use of human potential and the general philosophy is oriented around growth, expansion, flexibility, and risk-taking.

Miles and Snow (1978) explained that the *analyzer* type attempts to straddle both analyzer and defender types by taking the best of each and combining them into tactical plans. Pursuing an analyzer strategy requires a *blending* of the attributes of both prospector and defender. Between these two strategies, stability and innovation meet in equilibrium, mostly determined by environment changes and conditions; thus, analyzers capitalize where they can (Gimenez, 2000; Ingram et al., 2016; Miles et al., 1978; Parnell, 2002). A unique aspect of this strategy type is that it allows entrepreneurs to "watch their competitors closely for new ideas, and then they rapidly adopt those that appear to be most promising" (Gimenez, 2000, p. 238). Consequently, adaptation and flexibility come with risks. Miles et al. (1978) noted that the risks result from maintaining a balance between inefficiency and ineffectiveness among the dual purposes of pursuing environment opportunities and creating a stable structure that can withstand the gusts of environment and technological demands.

At the far end of the strategic spectrum is the *reactor* strategy, not a strategy *per se* (Miles & Snow, 1978). This strategy type is perceived as a non-strategy due to management inconsistency, incoherent direction, sluggish environment reactions, and less time and less effort spent on profitable pursuits. Unlike the other strategies, reactors focus more on short-term gains that only serve to play catch-up with competitors; otherwise, this type is apprehensive about changing directions in the face of environmental shifts (Ingram et al., 2016; Pleshko & Nickerson, 2008). Inertia is pervasive in this strategy type, especially related to capturing environment signals for necessary changes that can bolster the product/service. Increasing efficiency is the only objective for this type because there are no internal mechanisms to receive, interpret, and evaluate the environment signals that gauge when to adjust or diversify product/service offerings. The pursuit of a non-strategy occurs when other strategies have failed (Miles et al., 1978) and/or performed poorly when executed (Parnell, 2002).

To extend the subtle nature of the premise of the proposition in applying the Miles and Snow (1978) taxonomy, Matsuno and Mentzer (2000) suggested three relevant points of interest: (a) a firm's strategy decisions ought to be guided by the market, and environment signals, (b) a firm's strategy will ultimately drive a firm's performance indicators, and (c) a firm will be persistent in driving a performance indicator insofar as the strategy types are monotonic.

P₁: The Miles and Snow (1978) taxonomy is suitable for measuring firm-level strategy transitions. The applicability of this taxonomy shows the interactions of environmental variables reflecting the firm's decision to increase or decrease ACAP and whether to employ slack resources as the catalyst to transition from one strategy type to the next in response to the business environment.

Strategic Flexibility

When compared with large firms, strategy for small firms tends to be emergent, sporadic, and malleable due to the unstable nature of its business environment. Strategic flexibility is when firms reallocate resources to meet environmental demands or internal constraints based on consequential knowledge, leading to an increase in performance with the intent to adopt an unintended strategy. This theory underpins the main notion in the current study: firms move along the Miles and Snow (1978) taxonomy, employing slack and ACAP so that when entrepreneurs' adaptive strategies are in accordance with the nature of their intent, resources, actions, and investment strategies (Fernández-Pérez, del Mar Fuentes-Fuentes, & Bojana, 2012), they transition with flexibility.

The current research captures two unique aspects of strategic flexibility that are imperative to justify its use in the Miles and Snow (1978) taxonomy when (a) deploying resources toward competitiveness and (b) increasing the number of various patterns of resource deployment enabling flexibility. Three approaches are highlighted to justify and to support the claims made within this research: (a) flexible maneuvering of resources, (b) flexible process within a firm's operations, and (c) flexible cognitive approach of entrepreneurs, specifically the ability of entrepreneurs to maneuver strategies using internal resources as they see fit based on internal environment changes. This theory is multifaceted in that it can be applied at the firm level and individual level of analysis, which means resources are allocated or reallocated based on environment changes; at the decision-making level, the owner needs to have the strategic thinking skills to generate unorthodox tactics to maintain flexibility in strategic transition (Gross, 2016b). Because strategic flexibility is a dynamic capability (Grewal & Tansuhaj, 2001; Roberts & Stockport, 2009), it requires internal resources and conditions conducive to strategic transition.

Organizational slack resources and ACAP are two mechanisms by which a generic strategy under the Miles and Snow (1978) taxonomy can be executed. Matthyssens, Pauwels, and Vandenbempt (2005) identified three methods that increase strategic flexibility: (a) increase a firm's diversification strength, (b) invest in the firm's underutilized resources, and (c) reduce the commitment of resources that have been allocated.

Organizational Slack

Resources should be used to align with core capabilities, environment adaptations, or new product/service offerings. Shifts in the environment call for strategic thinking and actions by entrepreneurship to use excess resources to realize emerging strategic opportunities instead of as a tool for retaliation; consequently, this notion gives rise to the connection between slack resources and business strategy. De Falco and Renzi (2015) defined slack as "the amount of exceeding resources, eventually available for managerial discretionary use" (p. 168). Nohria and Gulati (1996) defined slack as "a pool of resource in an organization that is more than the minimum necessary to produce a given level of organizational output" (p. 1246). Herold, Jayaraman, and Narayanaswamy (2006) agreed, contending that slack is above and beyond standard requirements needed to meet firm-level objectives. Franquesa and Brandyberry (2009) acknowledged that no study in the business literature had addressed the multidimensional use of slack resources and a scarcity of evidence to support the effects of slack innovation in the firm.

Nohria and Gulati (1996) referred to slack resources as a cushion that can increase market share and carve out a new environment position. It can also be viewed as enabling wasteful habits or, more optimistically, a way to engage in innovative behavior (Herold et al., 2006). Bourgeois and Singh (1983) parceled slack into two main categories—absorbed and unabsorbed—and later added another category—potential slack. Many theorists have maintained there is a positive relationship between organizational slack resources and firm-level innovation (Chen & Huang, 2010; Cyert & March 1963; De Falco & Renzi, 2015; Herold et al., 2006; Nohria & Gulati, 1996). Supporters of the benefits of slack resources have listed the conditions for employing the effective use of slack in the functions of small firms (Franquesa & Brandyberry, 2009) Herold et al., 2006; Nohria & Gulati, 1996; Wefald et al., 2010).

Examples of slack resources are redundant employees, unused capacity, unused inventory, retained earnings, working capital, raised additional capital, and any unexplored opportunities that can increase output (Cyert & March 1963; Geoffrey Love & Nohria, 2005; Marlin & Geiger, 2015; Nohria & Gulati, 1996). Entrepreneurs can gain in the areas of process, goal orientation, promoting a culture of innovative behavior, and employee development by using slack. Experimentation with accumulated resources that would not have been used otherwise is encouraged, assuming the slack resources have not been absorbed; they are available and can be easily recovered (Franquesa & Brandyberry, 2009). Slack also allows for flexibility with environment adaptiveness, encouraging behaviors such as environmental scanning. Environmental scanning breeds new projects that entrepreneurs would be more willing to consider. It depends, of course, on whether the slack resource can be easily recovered versus slack that is least likely to be recovered because projects do fail.

The literature with a constrained view (narrow focus on environment penetration by staying within one environment product domain) of the influence of slack on firm-level innovation is replete with reasons and justifications as to the inherent nature of management decision-making there is access to resources. Nohria and Gulati (1996) shared an unconstrained view of slack resources and the use of slack for innovative purposes: "If slack is a form of inefficiency but also essential for innovation, organization runs the risk of eliminating slack to a point that undermines their capacity to innovate" (p. 1245). Slack resources encourage innovation: (a) slack produces a culture of experimentation in the form of a team, workgroup, or division; (b) slack is a safe method of testing new product environments and a justifiable means of tinkering with high-potential innovation by innovative champions; (c) with access to slack resources, entrepreneurs can psychologically take on more risk-inherent actions and exploration; (d) slack helps absorb technology; (e) slack brings fresh approaches or ideas that can be stored for a later date; and (f) slack can be a cushion in case a project fails.

P2: A firm's employment of slack resources impacts its ability to transition between strategies under the Miles and Snow (1978) taxonomy. Firms that do not employ slack resources follow a defender or reactor generic strategy; firms that employ slack resources transition toward a prospector strategy.

It is unclear how entrepreneurs acquire knowledge, assimilate knowledge, transfer knowledge, and exploit knowledge to expand strategic choices while maintaining sustainable competitive advantage. Muscio (2007) affirmed, "Little evidence has been provided about this important determinant of knowledge acquisition in the SMEs context" (p. 1). Grandinetti (2016) echoed this sentiment, asserting that there is a lack of "adequate theoretical and empirical research effort to analyze the role of relationships in an SME's knowledge management process" (p. 160).

The lack of practical understanding of ACAP at the firm level has hindered business practitioners' and academics' ability to understand the merits or demerits of ACAP (Flatten, Greve, & Brettel, 2011; Lane, Koka, & Pathak, 2006; Liao, Welsch, & Stoica, 2003). As a multidimensional construct related to business strategy adaptiveness ACAP literature has focused on large firms, albeit ACAP is an adequate construct to measure entrepreneurial business phenomena (Ahluwalia et al., 2017). The core of the ACAP construct is research and development—a minor activity in most firms. However, ACAP has not been measured in the context of smaller firms, resulting in major shortcomings in understanding ACAP impacts on strategy and strategic choice (Muscio, 2007). ACAP impacts strategic transition because it creates a responsive environment (through knowledge inflows and outflows) to either administrative, entrepreneurial, or engineering constraints in turbulent business landscapes (Escribano, Fosfuri, & Tribo, 2006).

Comprehensively, ACAP involves acquiring, assimilating, transforming, and exploiting new knowledge that directly or indirectly advances intrafirm or interfirm strategies (Gross, 2016a). ACAP is based on the seminal work of Cohen and Levin (1989) and Cohen and Levinthal (1990). Later, the ACAP dimensions were partitioned into two capabilities: potential and realized (Zahra &

George, 2002). The first level of ACAP is acquisition. Acquisition identifies and accumulates relevant knowledge to inject into a firm's operations to elicit positive consequences. Assimilation, the second level, includes and fuses a reinterpretation of knowledge that has been acquired externally. Transformation is the process of combining and refining existing knowledge to facilitate the altering of routines. Finally, the exploitation level is based on the routines and structure of the firm, whereby knowledge is applied to existing operations to commercialize new products or services.

In a breakthrough study, Cohen and Levinthal (1990) explained that firms with high levels of ACAP outperform firms with low ACAP. The concept of ACAP relates to product development and services initiated from acquired external knowledge gained for commercial ends. Gross (2016b) purported that knowledge gained externally is found in the external pockets of knowledge, consisting of suppliers, customers, competitors, and stakeholders. Gross proposed that firms that increase in ACAP are more likely to be entrepreneurial and have a greater propensity for taking risks, seeking innovativeness, and being proactive. The increase in entrepreneurial-orientated tactics happens over time from the accumulation of experience and resources it takes to acquire and to absorb knowledge from external sources and fuse it with existing knowledge within the firm—a lengthy process (Cohen & Levinthal, 1990; Grandinetti, 2016). These factors are vital to increasing firms' ACAP. Grandinetti (2016) and Cohen and Levinthal (1990) purported that the faster ACAP and relationships are cultivated, contacts coordinated, and actions implemented, the faster ACAP is increased.

To contribute to the vast amount of research in ACAP, a theoretical model is developed, and a framework is provided on the basis that along with organizational slack, ACAP is an important factor associated with the strategic transition. Unlike previous ACAP research, where the foci are on technical capabilities and entrepreneurial wealth (Deeds, 2001), managing knowledge for entrepreneurial growth (Gray, 2006), and human capital characteristics of the top echelon (Hayton & Zahra, 2005), the focus here is on the depth and intensity of ACAP on a firm's business strategy adaptation of any type whether prospector, analyzer, defender, or reactor. ACAP's influence on strategic choice seems *a priori*, but a further inquiry is needed in this domain.

P3:   A firm's intensity of ACAP impacts its ability to transition between strategies under the Miles and Snow (1978) taxonomy. If ACAP is inactive, firms follow a defender or reactor strategy type; if ACAP is active, firms transition toward a prospector strategy type.

Figures 1 and 2 explain the interaction between ACAP and organizational slack resources related to entrepreneurs making major strategic decisions that are transitory and adapt to firm-level environments. Figure 1 shows the overall view of these multifaced constructs while highlighting the push–pull environment dynamic. These interactions influence internal problems to be addressed (entrepreneurial, administrative, or engineering) at any given point in time and the adaptive strategy.

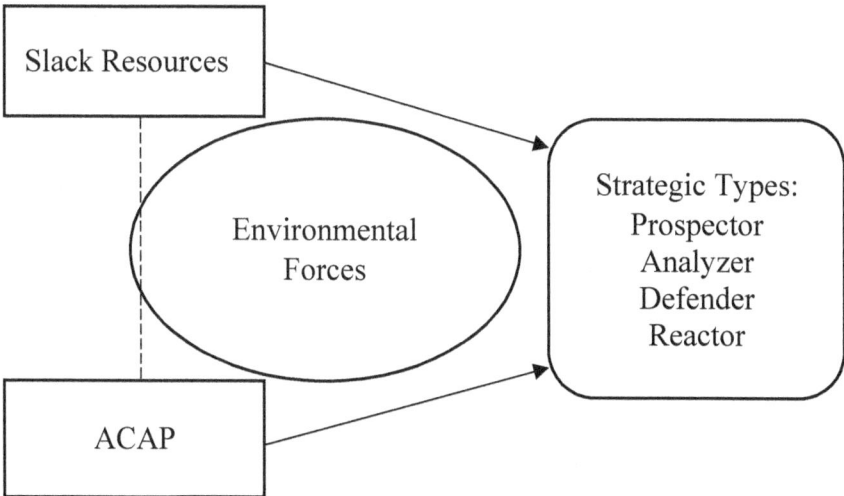

Figure 1. Relationship between slack and ACAP strategic type.

Figure 2 shows the strategic transitions as a spectrum that depends primarily on the degree of slack and ACAP applied to any given strategy decision; however, neither end of the spectrum is more advantageous than the other.

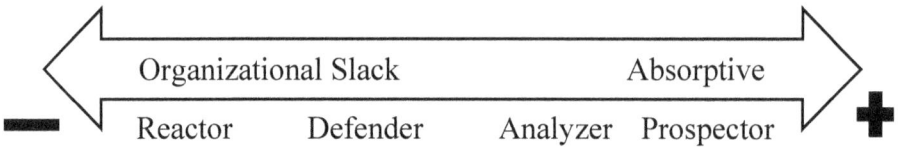

Figure 2. Slack/ACAP spectrum on strategic flexibility.

In many cases, using fewer slack resources is a matter of choice or personal philosophy. For example, a firm that maintains a defender position requires little to no need to seek and acquire new knowledge and assimilate it into the dynamic dominance of previously operative strategies. An owner may have a position where he or she has a sustainable competitive advantage at the industry level. Moreover, entrepreneurs who engage in new knowledge as appropriate to facilitate open innovation (Huang & Rice, 2009) expand entrepreneurially (Gray, 2006) or find ways to change during business landscape changes needed to modify their process perspective with available slack. This enables vertical and horizontal strategic dominance. At the far extremes are reactors. This group does not have the built-in mechanisms to receive environment signals that could alert them when to employ resources and knowledge to facilitate a strategic transition. As highlighted in Figure 1, the link between slack resources and ACAP does not exist in reactors. This is reinforced in Figure 2. The spectrum of usage of slack tends to decrease toward reactors but increases toward prospectors.

Slack Resources and Strategic Transition

Herold et al. (2006) used a series of patent-related data to inquire into the relationship between slack resources and innovation. They found a curvilinear relationship. The cause of this relationship, as they stated, was due to managerial behavior, which caused diminished returns on the slack resources. Chen and Huang (2010) examined the same variables and reported an inverse U-shaped relationship. This relationship was attributed to the different types of slack with unequal effects on innovative pursuits. These data were analyzed from a population of information technology managers, measuring their creativity in the workplace when slack was available. Geiger and Cashen (2002) sampled 228 companies and analyzed the data using regression analysis. They reported a positive, significant relationship between slack and innovation, which suggests that not only was optimizing slack usage impactful, but the type of slack and its application toward strategic ends was equally impactful.

Marlin and Geiger (2015), with a resource-based perspective, sampled 563 firms and 161 trade firms to examine the relationship between slack and firm-level performance. Marlin and Geiger suggested that slack resources and firm performance have a significant positive relationship. They showed that the configuration of slack increased firm-level outcomes and performance. If entrepreneurs decide to employ slack resources, they move along the strategic spectrum as either a prospector or an analyzer. These two strategy types require using slack to propel a firm into the frontier of innovation and increase performance. If entrepreneurs' position is to defend, then fewer slack resources are employed. These entrepreneurs view slack from a constrained perspective. Defending types' foci might assume this strategy based on internal conflicts related to absorbing environment signals, a new knowledge base, or knowledge assimilation constraints.

The use of slack resources has been a contentious discourse among academics and practitioners. Entrepreneurs' application of slack to pursue a prospecting or analyzer strategy means that slack must be increasingly used. A firm's ability to effectively use slack resources has been linked to innovation, which ties in with the prospector and analyzer (contingency) types. Bourgeois (1981) and Cyert and March (1963) concluded that slack resources help explain organizational behavior, particularly in gaining insight to reduce interfirm goal conflict, promoting political behavior, and driving strategic phenomena. Slack is a facilitator of strategic behavior and strategic thinking.

ACAP and Strategic Transition

Flatten et al. (2011) reported a positive relationship between firm-level ACAP and performance that influences firm-level competitive advantage to a large degree. Lichtenthaler and Lichtenthaler (2009) maintained that a strong link between ACAP and open innovation was causative and associative with firm-level growth strategies. Escribano et al. (2009) sampled 2,265 firms using survey instrumentation measuring the effects of ACAP as a moderating variable on competitive advantage in tumultuous business landscapes. They suggested that firms with higher ACAP are better at identifying external knowledge inflows but can maintain a competitive position in competitive business environments. Some business entrepreneurs do not intend to defend an environment position; rather, they prefer to seek knowledge and create inflow possibilities (Escribano et al., 2009).

Kostopoulos, Papalexandris, Papachroni, and Ioannou (2011) agreed with previous research findings that ACAP is an antecedent to innovation and positively impacted financial performance when mediated by external knowledge inflows. Matusik and Heeley (2005) sampled 112 firms using survey instrumentation and found a positive relationship between ACAP dimensions (acquisition, assimilation, transformation, and exploitation) and knowledge creation of employees within the firm. They added that newcomers' tacit knowledge plays a vital role in intensifying ACAP. It also adds that moderate turnover promotes the internal exploration of existing routines and structures that might have gone unnoticed due to inertia.

In a somewhat related study, Matsuno and Mentzer (2000) sampled 1,000 marketing executives out of a total of 3,300 manufacturing firms based on a list culled by the researchers. They reported that strategy type, as a moderating variable, was related to market orientation and economic performance. Firms with a market-oriented approach tend to use information and knowledge relevant to the pursuit of advantageous market activities. This finding, among others they purported, is encouraging because no such study has shown the link between strategy types and market activities.

These findings indicate that ACAP dimensions are related to business entrepreneurs' strategic flexibility and transition abilities under the Miles and Snow (1978) taxonomy. However, if ACAP is intensified, then firms reap the benefits of a prospecting position in the environment. The analyzer type, unlike the other three strategic types, could intensify ACAP if the decision is to transition to either a defensive or prospecting position; however, the prospecting type maintains a constant inward flow of knowledge and sustains structures that can assimilate transmutable knowledge and thereby transform it to meet the needs of strategy transition. To that end, strategy adaptiveness and the transition is positively associated with ACAP. Relatedly, a defender type of firm might acquire consequential knowledge from external sources and transform that knowledge with the intention of making an upward transition toward an analyzer type. Firms with massive inflows of knowledge can make strategic transitions easily and rapidly compared with firms that cannot absorb inflows. Businesses that reap the benefits of high-intensity ACAP can experiment with assimilation and transformation to ensure a direction of sustainable competitive advantage and generic strategic transition.

CONCLUSION

The current research attempted to reinterpret the Miles and Snow (1978) taxonomy for several reasons. This research adds theory development and points of interest for future endeavors based on the following: (a) a new view of the Miles and Snow taxonomy as a transitory process requiring strategic flexibility and strategy types based on business environment; (b) the taxonomy has not been examined in the domain of SME strategy-making literature, and (c) in terms of strategy, two internal factors have been unreported in the literature—the impact of slack resources and ACAP and their relation to the firm strategy type. While many studies have suggested that resources are important to strategy, none of them has explicitly reported the types of resources or number of resources needed to transition the firm's business strategy under the Miles and

Snow taxonomy. In many ways, ACAP is a factor to increase performance and cultivate innovative behaviors that direct a course of strategy. Few studies have measured this phenomenon or linked it to a positive or negative association to strategic adaptation at the firm level of analysis. This is especially the case for knowledge inflows, outflows, assimilation of knowledge, transformation for internal fit, and possible exploration as a transitionary mechanism to move along the Miles and Snow taxonomy.

Three propositions were provided for the continuation of future research endeavors to measure these variables, where the results can be added to the mosaic of literature on business enterprises. This research was conducted to link two internal resource-based resources as drivers of strategy adaptation based on the Miles and Snow (1978) taxonomy. Therefore, it is recommended that future studies employ quantitative methods to measure both slack and ACAP in an entrepreneurial business setting. It would be advantageous if context could be diversified, whereby researchers incorporate medium-sized firms and perhaps a particular cultural segment to be comparatively examined. Future research might parcel out each of the strategy types to see if their make-up is contingent on external or internal factors. For example, the defender type is one in which internal efficiency is traded up for a narrow market product or service offering; the defender's efficiency should be tested to measure if, in fact, this strategy type is in harmony with its description.

REFERENCES

Ahluwalia, S., Mahto, R. V., & Walsh, S. T. (2017). Innovation in small firms: Does family vs. non-family matter? *Journal of Small Business Strategy, 27*(3), 39-49.

Alfirević, N., Pavičić, J., & Gnjidić, V. (2014). Cognitive structure, managers' shared social understanding: From psychological and sociological concepts to managerial strategic choices. *Zagreb International Review of Economics and Business, 17*(2), 83-96.

Barney, J. B. (1986). Strategic factor markets: Expectations, luck, and business strategy. *Management Science, 32*(10), 1231-1241.

Barney, J. B. (1991). Firm resources and sustained competitive advantage. *Journal of Management, 17*(1), 99-120.

Bourgeois, L. J. (1981). On the measurement of organizational slack. *Academy of Management Review, 6*(1), 29-39.

Bourgeois, L. J., & Singh, J. V. (1983, August). Organizational slack and political behavior among top management teams. *Academy of Management Proceedings. Academy of Management, 1*, 43-47. Retrieved from http://proceedings.aom.org/content/1983/1/43.short

Burgelman, R. A. (2005). The role of strategy making in organizational evolution. *From Resource Allocation to Strategy*, 38-70.

Chandler, A. D. (1962). *Strategy and structure: Chapters in the history of the American enterprise*. Cambridge: Massachusetts Institute of Technology.

Chen, C. J., & Huang, Y. F. (2010). Creative workforce density, organizational slack, and innovation performance. *Journal of Business Research, 63*(4), 411-417.

Cohen, W. M., & Levin, R. C. (1989). Empirical studies of innovation and market structure. *Handbook of Industrial Organization, 2*, 1059-1107.

Cohen, W. M., & Levinthal, D. A. (1990). Absorptive capacity: A new perspective on learning and innovation. *Administrative Science Quarterly*, 128-152.

Cyert, R. M., & March, J. G. (1963). *A behavioral theory of the firm*. Englewood Cliffs, NJ: Prentice-Hall.

Deeds, D. L. (2001). The role of R&D intensity, technical development and absorptive capacity in creating entrepreneurial wealth in high technology start-ups. *Journal of Engineering and Technology Management, 18*(1), 29-47.

De Falco, S. E., & Renzi, A. (2015). The role of sunk cost and slack resources in innovation: A conceptual reading in an entrepreneurial perspective. *Entrepreneurship Research Journal*, 5(3), 167-179.

Desarbo, W., Di Benedetto, A., Song, M., & Sinha, I. J. (2005). Extending the Miles and Snow strategic framework: Strategic types, capabilities, environmental uncertainty, and firm performance. *Strategic Management Journal, 26*(1), 47-74.

Ensign, P. C. (2008). Small business strategy as a dynamic process: Concepts, controversies, and implications. *Journal of Business and Entrepreneurship, 20*(2), 25.

Escribano, A., Fosfuri, A., & Tribo, J. A. (2006). Managing external knowledge flows: The moderating role of absorptive capacity. *Research Policy, 38*(1), 96-105.

Fernández-Pérez, V., del Mar Fuentes-Fuentes, M., & Bojica, A. (2012). Strategic flexibility and change: The impact of social networks. *Journal of Management & Organization, 18*(1), 2-15.

Feurer, R., & Chaharbaghi, K. (1994). Defining competitiveness: A holistic approach. *Management Decision, 32*(2), 49-58.

Fiss, P. C. (2011). Building better causal theories: A fuzzy set approach to typologies in organization research. *Academy of Management Journal, 54*(2), 393-420.

Flatten, T. C., Greve, G. I., & Brettel, M. (2011). Absorptive capacity and firm performance in SMEs: The mediating influence of strategic alliances. *European Management Review, 8*(3), 137-152.

Franquesa, J., & Brandyberry, A. (2009). Organizational slack and information technology innovation adoption in SMEs. *International Journal of E-Business Research, 5*(1), 25-48. doi:10.4018/jebr.2009010102.

Geiger, S. W., & Cashen, L. H. (2002). A multidimensional examination of slack and its impact on innovation. *Journal of Managerial Issues*, 68-84.

Geoffrey Love, E., & Nohria, N. (2005). Reducing slack: The performance consequences of downsizing by large industrial firms, 1977-93. *Strategic Management Journal, 26*(12), 1087-1108.

Gimenez, F. A. (2000). The benefits of a coherent strategy for innovation and corporate change: A study applying Miles and Snow's model in the context of small firms. *Creativity and Innovation Management,* 9(4), 235-244.

Grandinetti, R. (2016). Absorptive capacity and knowledge management in small and medium enterprises. *Knowledge Management & Practice,* 2(14), 159-168.

Gray, C. (2006). Absorptive capacity, knowledge management and innovation in entrepreneurial small firms. *International Journal of Entrepreneurial Behavior & Research,* 12(6), 345-360.

Grewal, R., & Tansuhaj, P. (2001). Building organizational capabilities for managing economic crisis: The role of market orientation and strategic flexibility. *Journal of Marketing,* 65(2), 67-80.

Gross, R. (2016a). Exploring the moderating impact of absorptive capacity on strategic thinking, innovative behavior, and entrepreneurial orientation at the organizational level of analysis. *Journal of Management Policy and Practice,* 18(3), 60-83.

Gross, R. (2016b). Towards an understanding of the relationship between leadership styles and strategic thinking: A small and medium enterprise perspective. *Journal of Business Studies Quarterly,* 8(2), 22-39.

Hambrick, D. C. (1983). Some tests of the effectiveness and functional attributes of Miles and Snow's strategic types. *Academy of Management Journal,* 26(1), 5-26.

Hart, S. L. (1992). An integrative framework for strategy-making processes. *Academy of Management Review,* 17(2), 327-351.

Hayton, J. C., & Zahra, S. A. (2005). Venture team human capital and absorptive capacity in high technology new ventures. *International Journal of Technology Management,* 31(3-4), 256-274.

Herold, D. M., Jayaraman, N., & Narayanaswamy, C. R. (2006). What is the relationship between organizational slack and innovation? *Journal of Managerial Issues,* 372-392.

Huang, F., & Rice, J. (2009). The role of absorptive capacity in facilitating "open innovation" outcomes: A study of Australian SMEs in the manufacturing sector. *International Journal of Innovation Management, 13*(02), 201-220.

Ingram, T., Kraśnicka, T., Wronka-Pośpiech, M., Głód, G., & Głód, W. (2016). Relationships between Miles and Snow strategic types and organizational performance in Polish production companies. *Journal of Management and Business Administration, 24*(1), 17-45.

Kerin, R. A., Varadarajan, P. R., & Peterson, R. A. (1992). First-mover advantage: A synthesis, conceptual framework, and research propositions. *The Journal of Marketing*, 33-52.

Kostopoulos, K., Papalexandris, A., Papachroni, M., & Ioannou, G. (2011). Absorptive capacity, innovation, and financial performance. *Journal of Business Research, 64*(12), 1335-1343.

Kotey, B., & Meredith, G. G. (1997). Relationships among owner/manager personal values, business strategies, and enterprise performance. *Journal of Small Business Management, 35*(2), 37.

Lane, P. J., Koka, B. R., & Pathak, S. (2006). The reification of absorptive capacity: A critical review and rejuvenation of the construct. *Academy of Management Review, 31*(4), 833-863.

Liao, J., Welsch, H., & Stoica, M. (2003). Organizational absorptive capacity and responsiveness: An empirical investigation of growth–oriented SMEs. *Entrepreneurship Theory and practice, 28*(1), 63-86.

Lichtenthaler, U., & Lichtenthaler, E. (2009). A capability-based framework for open innovation: Complementing absorptive capacity. *Journal of Management Studies, 46*(8), 1315-1338.

Marlin, D., & Geiger, S. W. (2015). A reexamination of the organizational slack and innovation relationship. *Journal of Business Research, 68*(12), 2683-2690.

Matsuno, K., & Mentzer, J. T. (2000). The effects of strategy type on the market orientation-performance relationship. *Journal of Marketing, 64*(4), 1-16.

Matthyssens, P., Pauwels, P., & Vandenbempt, K. (2005). Strategic flexibility, rigidity and barriers to the development of absorptive capacity in business environments: Themes and research perspectives. *Industrial Marketing Management, 34*(6), 547-554.

Matusik, S. F., & Heeley, M. B. (2005). Absorptive capacity in the software industry: Identifying dimensions that affect knowledge and knowledge creation activities. *Journal of Management, 31*(4), 549-572.

McDaniel, S. W., & Kolari, J. W. (1987). Marketing strategy implications of the Miles and Snow strategic typology. *The Journal of Marketing*, 19-30.

Miles, R. E., Snow, C. C., Meyer, A. D., & Coleman Jr, H. J. (1978). Organizational strategy, structure, and process. *Academy of management review, 3*(3), 546-562.

Miles, R. E., & Snow, C. C. (1986). Organizations: New concepts for new forms. *California Management Review, 28*(3), 62-73.

Miles, R. E., Snow, C. C., Meyer, A. D., & Coleman, H. J. (1978). Organizational strategy, structure, and process. *Academy of Management Review, 3*(3), 546-562.

Mintzberg, H. (1994). The fall and rise of strategic planning. *Harvard Business Review, 72*(1), 107-114.

Mintzberg, H., & McHugh, A. (1985). Strategy formation in an adhocracy. *Administrative Science Quarterly*, 160-197.

Mintzberg, H., & Westley, F. (1992). Cycles of organizational change. *Strategic Management Journal, 13*(S2), 39-59.

Muscio, A. (2007). The impact of absorptive capacity on SMEs' collaboration. *Economics of Innovation and New Technology, 16*(8), 653-668.

Nohria, N., & Gulati, R. (1996). Is slack good or bad for innovation? *Academy of Management Journal, 39*(5), 1245-1264.

Nyberg, A., Reilly, G., Essman, S., & Rodrigues, J. (2017). Human capital resources: A call to retire settled debates and to start a few new debates. *The International Journal of Human Resource Management*, 1-19.

Olson, S. F., & Currie, H. M. (1992). Female entrepreneurs: Personal value systems and business strategies in a male-dominated industry. *Journal of Small Business Management, 30*(1), 49.

O'Regan, N., & Ghobadian, A. (2004). Innovation in SMEs: The impact of strategic orientation and environmental perceptions. *International Journal of Productivity and Performance Management, 54*(2), 81-97.

Parnell, J. A. (2002). Competitive strategy research: Current challenges and new directions. *Journal of Management Research, 2*(1), 1.

Pettigrew, A. M. (1992). On studying managerial elites. *Strategic Management Journal, 13*(S2), 163-182.

Pleshko, L., & Nickerson, I. (2008). Strategic orientation, organizational structure, and the associated effects on performance in industrial firms. *Academy of Strategic Management Journal, 7*, 95.

Porter, M. E. (1980). Industry structure and competitive strategy: Keys to profitability. *Financial Analysts Journal, 36*(4), 30-41.

Raymond, L., & Bergeron, F. (2008). Enabling the business strategy of SMEs through e-business capabilities: A strategic alignment perspective. *Industrial Management & Data Systems, 108*(5), 577-595.

Roberts, N., & Stockport, G. J. (2009). Defining strategic flexibility. *Global Journal of Flexible Systems Management, 10*(1), 27.

Robins, J., & Wiersema, M. F. (1995). A resource-based approach to the multibusiness firm: Empirical analysis of portfolio interrelationships and corporate financial performance. *Strategic Management Journal, 16*(4), 277-299.

Shortell, S. M., & Zajac, E. J. (1990). Perceptual and archival measures of Miles and Snow's strategic types: A comprehensive assessment of reliability and validity. *Academy of Management Journal, 33*(4), 817-832.

Srour, M., Baird, K., & Schoch, H. (2016). The role of strategic flexibility in the associations between management control system characteristics and strategic change. *Contemporary Management Research, 12*(3), 371.

Tang, Z., & Tang, J. (2012). Entrepreneurial orientation and SME performance in China's changing environment: The moderating effects of strategies. *Asia Pacific Journal of Management, 29*(2), 409-431.

Verreynne, M. L., & Meyer, D. (2010). Small business strategy and the industry life cycle. *Small Business Economics, 35*(4), 399-416.

Wefald, A. J., Katz, J. P., Downey, R. G., & Rust, K. G. (2010). Organizational slack, firm performance, and the role of industry. *Journal of Managerial Issues*, 70-87.

Zahra, S. A., & George, G. (2002). Absorptive capacity: A review, reconceptualization, and extension. *Academy of Management Review, 27*(2), 185-203.

Zahra, S. A., & Pearce, J. A. (1990). Research evidence on the Miles-Snow typology. *Journal of Management, 16*(4), 751-768.

Zhou, K. Z., & Wu, F. (2010). Technological capability, strategic flexibility, and product innovation. *Strategic Management Journal, 31*(5), 547-561.

Chapter 7:
Entrepreneurial Leadership and
High-Velocity Markets

This chapter presents a new theoretical perspective on absorptive capacity (ACAP) and its nexus between entrepreneurial leadership and innovation patterns in high-velocity markets. High-velocity markets have five main characteristics: rapid-fire technological changes, short product life cycles, rapidly evolving customer expectations, frequent launches of new competitive moves, and the entry of critical new rivals. Firms operating in high-velocity markets have significant innovative imperatives than firms that operate in nonvolatile markets.

Under certain market conditions, knowledge and innovative pattern trajectories may change based on the internal knowledge intake and assimilation of that knowledge to harness marketplace opportunities. Firms operating in high-velocity markets rely on knowledge that can be realized and transmitted in conjunction with entrepreneurial decision-making.

INTRODUCTION

Faced with many challenges congruent with opportunities, a firm reacts to a continuous advent of technological advances and operating methods in a market economy. The present market economy's reality is that products and other technology iterations and quick-to-market activities are happening to a much greater degree in high-velocity markets. The past does not represent what the future will bring. However, an internal process of ACAP makes future decision-making for entrepreneurial leaders useful in the long run. The caveat is a variety of firms that operate in high-velocity markets, where decisions are posed and executed in the short run. However, firms have a natural tendency to take advantage of economies of scale or scope through futuristic means to sustain themselves in high-velocity markets in the long run. *Does the entrepreneurial leadership of a firm adjust the innovation patterns from rigidity to fluidity based on knowledge acquisition, or do they attempt to break away from established innovation patterns?*

Firms in high-velocity environments can grow, adapt, and perform at the highest speed to market (Srikanth & Mohanavel, 2017). This comment is timely and helps examine the connection between knowledge and innovation patterns. Additionally, this comment explores the consequences of ACAP on entrepreneurial decision-making and the discontinuous or continuous innovation patterns (IP) in the context of high-velocity markets. High-velocity markets "render imprecise, unavailable or obsolete information at the disposal of firms to formulate their strategy, thus generating a high degree of uncertainty to be dealt with" (Srikanth & Mohanavel, 2017, p. 2), which aligns with the motivation for this comment.

Additionally, strategic planning in the conventional sense poses quite well the challenge for entrepreneurial leaders in markets and industries characterized as high-velocity (Wirtz, Mathieu, & Schilke, 2007). For this reason, the current chapter provides a new way of understanding the effects of knowledge, the knowledge problem, and how ACAP never gets to equilibrium (i.e., the supply of external knowledge acquired at the level needed and then converted internally) due to its perpetual motion in high-paced environments. Moreover, the perspective of this comment elucidates the notion that strategic planning should be viewed as a process that includes new knowledge and assimilation methods that eventually serve commercialization and, as a result, embeds the entrepreneurial elements. Planning in the conventional sense removes the entrepreneurial element, which dismisses new knowledge that can change the nature of a firm's innovation patterns. With this, entrepreneurial leaders have to decide on the knowledge that will affect the long-run IP in the short run. This view remains unaddressed in the management and strategic literature. Therefore, the high-velocity market strategy that serves as the underpinning for explaining the consequences of ACAP is proactiveness, replication, and reconfiguration. Abernathy and Utterback (1978) were the frontrunners of categorizing IP.

Abernathy and Utterback (1978) categorized IP as fluid, transitional, or specific. ACAP, at any rate, or flow, seems to require IP to switch and adjust from either a state of rigidity or fluidity of process or product. To ascertain the connection between high-velocity markets and IP and understand this view, Oliver (2012) said, "High-velocity markets make existing resources, capabilities and core competencies less relevant and less likely to yield competitive advantage. These resources need to be reconfigured, renewed, refreshed and adapted for superior firm performance" (p. 4).

LITERATURE REVIEW

The current inquiry into the nexus between IP and entrepreneurial leaders' decisions has not been examined in the management or strategy literature. Entrepreneurial leadership (EL) has been elucidated in previous studies on its effect on the innovating firm, especially within the operation of the flexible firm. A derivative of entrepreneurial behavior is innovation and observable IP. This comment assumes that ACAP influences EL and IP. The influence of ACAP changes the trajectory of the S-curve pattern of firms. As the firm absorbs and realizes potential knowledge, it can severely impact its future course of action. Knowledge is either organizational (i.e., soft) or technical (i.e., hard).

The main assumption is that the firm's EL is the purveyor of innovation, establishing patterns. The synthesizer of the resources needed to carry out innovation within the firm's confines is motivated by knowledge. Carl Menger (2007) stated, "Nothing is more certain than that the degree of economic progress of mankind will still, in the future epochs, be commensurate with the degree of progress of human knowledge" (p. 74). This refers to the need for knowledge and the importance of knowledge in the market economy. This chapter couches knowledge (i.e., ACAP) within the firm's imperative nature and seeks to explain how the firm's individuals acquire knowledge and employ it in high-velocity firms. The market response and adjustment of a firm to high-velocity market demands exemplify the decision-making unit's ability to employ EL capabilities (Eisenhardt & Martin, 2000).

These comments focus on connecting a firm's ACAP influences on EL decision-making, which changes the firm's trajectory of IP, thereby creating upward pressure on its S-curve. Thus, ACAP pushes the S-curve of the firm's products and technologies over and across the chasm, beyond the parameters of performance and effort. In any case, ACAP has consequential effects on the firm to push the S-curve across the chasm, directly influencing EL decision-making. When individuals acquire knowledge from various external pockets, it changes the data and the conditions of future strategies related to IP. Coincidentally, the firm does not hold the memory of learning or knowledge; the firm's individuals hold memory and learn from the market. Cohen and Levinthal (1990) agreed, "An organization's absorptive capacity will depend on the absorptive capacities of its members" (p. 131). This comment is organized around six research questions while the context is theoretical.

The current chapter intends to theoretically explain the managerial and strategic management literature to draw distinctive points about ACAP and determine its propensity to be entrepreneurial, innovative, and competitive. Furthermore, it highlights that when ACAP is obtained, assimilated, and exploited in high-velocity markets, it has variable effects on a firm's S-curve. This process is postulated as the shifter of the firm's S-curve IP. A series of market phenomena have indicated noticeable IP shifts: phonograph, airplane, telephone, and computer television. Den Hertog and Bilderbeek (1999) agreed that service IP and product IP differ in their visibility. ACAP, too, is invisible but can manifest itself in the production factors in developing a product. The knowledge floating in various market ecosystems via market participants is harnessed through its market mechanisms and employed to pursue market ends. The firm-level analysis has either expert or mundane knowledge that can transmute the firm's direction, only if it is not unconditionally locked into a strategic choice predating a new circumstance. Individuals and firms reward the best use of these knowledge bases acquired by market mechanisms, ultimately deciding what is and is not needed.

However, there is a tendency to view knowledge as static or spontaneous. Hayek (1945) expressed that knowledge is uneven and decentralized— firms included. No given amount of knowledge is held by any one individual. Hayek was one of the first economists to use and explain the categorization of knowledge as either tacit or mundane. Organizational learning can be a continuous and complicated process for individuals within the firm (Lindsey & Norman, 1977). However, individuals use their knowledge along with ideas to pursue novel innovation (Schumpeter, 1934). Innovation happens due to the external market movements of economic change. An overlooked point related to learning from the market process is the fits and starts that Schumpeter (1934) expressed as a rotating and irregular occurrence; the same is true of internal *potential* and *realized* learned capabilities. Firms respond to market signals, attempting to find profit opportunities amid market distortions.

Entrepreneurial leaders acquire knowledge through prices, customers, suppliers, and competitors. The entrepreneurial type of leadership learns from within and from without the firm. Although there is a growing understanding of organizational flexibility's emergent nature, there is little clarity about the consequences of ACAP and assimilation of said knowledge to affect IP. Making decisions in high-velocity markets demands information and knowledge of the market. It also requires the decision-making capacity to use the transmutation, assimilation, and commercialization of that knowledge to apply to emerging innovation (Childs, 2015).

Information and knowledge are critical to a firm's survival (i.e., profit or loss, competitiveness, market position, and strategy) in high-velocity markets because EL's use market signals to make judgments about using future resources so that ideas might become commercialized. The knowledge floating in various markets is harnessed through the market mechanisms and provides means to market ends. That knowledge is used to make decisions on the direction, targets, and strategic positioning of resources. This is not so much an individual result but individuals' combined effect within a firm's use of knowledge bases as observed by market signals that decide what is and what is not worth pursuing.

However, there is a tendency to view knowledge as static and not as a continuous flow. High-velocity markets are unique in that they are volatile, uncertain, and experience unpredicted waves of uncertainty. Firms in such a market must be adaptable to change and rapid product and service deployment. High-velocity market conditions allow firms to adapt in the most effective way to sustain business in the long term (Oliver, 2016). For these reasons, the technology S-curve is used as a yardstick for tracing the effects of ACAP and its diffuse effects on firm-level IP. Diffusion S-curves are not all the same in what they model. Therefore, this comment seeks to focus on the technology S-curve primarily because of its characteristics, which are constructed based on performance and effort due to the prospect of product and technological propensity to encounter diminishing performance over time.

High-Velocity and Innovation Patterns

Along with other essential terms in economics and later in management and strategic management is innovation—the propensity to innovate within the firm and in the ongoing internal process of ACAP that enables innovation to flourish within the firm. The term *innovation* helps explain individual behavior and its market response to new market data and competitive pressures (Schumpeter, 1964). High-velocity environments exist in market economies where firms position for market share, resource scarcity, knowledge costs, and configuring lag and lead time for innovative methods of production and growth-related projects raised within the firm.

The firm's lag and lead times to innovation are critical to gaining market share because of the rapid customer and industry data changes in relation to space and time. Carl Menger (2007), the founder of Austrian economics, once said, "All change consists of nothing but differences through time" (p. 122). That is, data changes through time; and production takes time, which changes the stock of knowledge related to innovation as a competitive tool in high-velocity markets. Furthermore, competitiveness is more pronounced in high-velocity firms than in traditional industry structures where time is not essential. The innovation process involves knowledge-oriented processes and resource-use processes that bring an idea to fruition. Knowledge-based processes are the vital capabilities of firms in high-velocity markets. These capabilities dictate the IP that establishes what a firm can and cannot pursue at a given cycle (i.e., fast, stable, and slow). Many resources go into making strategy and implementing resources to their most urgent uses based on demand. However, the question here is how to use it and formulate the knowledge into new processes.

How does the firm's ACAP affect a firm's innovation patterns, from slow to accelerated, and the entrepreneurial response from leadership at any given time? While resources are essential, knowledge costs are imperative to IP development. EL, otherwise known as purveyors of innovative patterns and resources, would be either positively or adversely affected by a firm's IP if ACAP alters in any way. It is one thing to choose a set of market options based on observable indicators (competition, pricing, technological advancements, and new products); it is a whole other process to choose from unknown and unrealizable observational indicators. Entrepreneurial leaders base their assumptions on market indicators that are known and some that emerge. Market indicators of innovative options are known as either target or strategic reference points within the market cycle. However, how do these options derail or direct IP? For the most part, IP relies on the contextual, timely, and error-free knowledge transmitted to entrepreneurial leaders at any point in time to make strategic innovation decisions. These decisions imply that the knowledge needed to make innovation and technological advancement must be somewhat defined to be employed.

ACAP is a non-neutral function. Wherever the knowledge gets injected into the firm, it is likely to be the catalyst for changes in how knowledge is realized, exploited, and transformed into useable market responses. Is there a concentrated benefit to the firm that initiates new knowledge to be later exploited? Are the costs of acquired new knowledge spread throughout the firm to later be commercialized?

This comment is timely. As firms recognize and assimilate internal and external knowledge to pursue goals and strategic aims, it becomes imperative to advance innovation. Knowledge, coupled with externally derived sources from market pockets, has been theorized as having a moderating effect on firms' strategic actions (Gross, 2017, 2018). Nevertheless, there is little understanding of ACAP consequences on IP and entrepreneurial leaders' strategic decision-making in the context of high-velocity markets. Even less is mentioned in the strategic literature about the assimilated knowledge and exploited as forces create upward pressure on a firm's S-curve pattern.

Firms in high-velocity markets change IP. Path A is chosen one moment, then Path B is chosen, and so on, thus changing the nature of paths (flexibility). The probability of success is acknowledged only through the lens of crossing the innovation chasm due to increased performance and effort. The axis of the technology S-curve represents the performance and effort of a technological product. Nevertheless, here, there is a suggestion that the axis represents time and knowledge as innovation paths are pursued. Just because there is a formulated innovative path does not mean it ought to be or should be brought to market.

Ludwig von Mises (1956) helped with the notion, stating,

> Changes in technological knowledge and in the demand of consumers as they occur daily in our time make obsolete many of the plans directing the course of production and raise the question whether or not one should pursue the path stated. (p. 502)

A firm's paths often change in dynamic markets and are determined by the flow of ACAP. Technically, there will always be a knowledge problem regarding its employability under specific firm capabilities due to market and internal constraints. However, the focus is on the process and effect of that learning in determining IP, particularly in markets characterized as high velocity, including those firms that make constant and deliberate adjustments to market conditions.

Again, this chapter intends to theoretically examine the managerial and strategic management literature to draw distinctive points related to a non-neutral injection of ACAP. ACAP determines the firm's propensity to be entrepreneurial, innovative, and competitive, but ultimately it shows that ACAP is obtained, assimilated, and exploited and can alter and disrupt IP. There is a tendency to view ACAP in a linear function—knowledge is externally assimilated to commercialization. There is much agreement on the vital role of knowledge management (Rai, 2011), where new knowledge may have a ripple effect on existing IP. Presented here is the contrary thesis: knowledge that has been acquired externally, based on the needs of the firm, minus market distortions, might change the innovation pattern and entrepreneurial decision-making.

Simply, does the firm continue with old plans with new knowledge or change pattern with new knowledge, and to what degree does innovation patterns change over time? Externally derived knowledge is critical to a firm's innovative capabilities (Cohen & Levinthal, 1990). One of the ACAP points overlooked the firm's prior knowledge and future knowledge differential, *post ante* acquisition of other market-based knowledge pieces. Cohen and Levinthal (1990) stated, "Prior related knowledge confer[s] an ability to recognize the value of new information, assimilate it, and apply it to commercial ends" (p. 128). The two main factors of ACAP are potential and realized capabilities. What was not included in Cohen and Levinthal's assertion is how external knowledge acquisition has a wavy, circular-like movement. The firm's external market-based knowledge and the exploitation of said knowledge affect its propensity for innovation.

As Cohen and Levinthal (1990) outlined, ACAP has four dimensions: *potential* (acquisition and assimilation) and *realized* (transformation and exploitation). How does ACAP affect the propensity of innovation? How does ACAP affect a firm's strategic choice in high-velocity markets? A firm has given aims and goals for the future. To accomplish them, the firm uses resources from the factors of production. Typically, firms develop strategies based on known targets, market positions, or market-based objectives. However, the mainstream literature goes unnoticed because a firm's aims, targets, or objectives are mostly unseen. Firms create market change, which is a characteristic of high-velocity markets. The ACAP process, as we know of it conceptually, does not in any way account for error. There is no way to predict the new entrants, new rivals, or customer changes in expectations as these variables change rapidly. This poses a knowledge problem for many firms trying to decide what is useful or useless for any given market strategic trajectory. Decisions are made based on the market's coordinating mechanism, albeit exchanges between individuals and between firms. More importantly, the unseen heightens the level of error of ACAP. The simple fact is that there is not enough knowledge in the general framework of a market economy and the ability to make sense of it in any space and time.

To date, no strategic model exists that accounts for error or that illustrates a need to account for errors in EL strategic decision-making. Strategic models do not and have not accounted for errors in choice or error within ACAP. Although there are many analytical managerial tools, the inescapable imperative in a market economy is the absence of error. It attempts to give rise to the present and long-term consequences of working and planning in error related to the two main factors of ACAP (*realized* and *unrealized capacity*). Individuals carry out their plans in the marketplace. However, these are based on the expectations that others will conduct their plans under the same set of circumstances and knowledge related to ELs within firms. A learning organization continuously engages in the complex process (Lindsey & Norman, 1977) of the acquisition and use of error-prone knowledge. However, entrepreneurial leaders use a multitude of learning related to innovative knowledge. Some knowledge inflow and spillover effects have *fits* and *starts* due to external economic changes and market movements (Schumpeter, 1935). An overlooked point related to ACAP from market knowledge is the fits and starts that Schumpeter (1935) expressed as a rotating and irregular occurrence; the same is true of internal *potential* and *realized* learned capabilities.

Firms respond to market signals and ultimately attempt to find profit opportunities amid market distortions. In this way, ACAP responds to the market with data as firms learn something new. This changes the use and need of various internal capabilities. Firms may find pressure in the market to acquire knowledge instead of learning by doing, which is the critical aspect of keeping abreast of industry developments and requires adjustments to market investment. This type of knowledge, however, is prevalent in high-velocity markets.

P₁: ACAP negatively affects a firm's entrepreneurial decision and IP.

P₂: ACAP positively affects a firm's entrepreneurial decision-making and IP.

Entrepreneurial Leadership

EL is rooted in both leadership and entrepreneurial thought. Entrepreneurship has been noted in several economic theorists, such as Schumpeter, Mises, Kirzner, Marshall, and Cantillon—just to name a few. On the other hand, leadership is one of the most widely studied phenomena related to the dynamic between two or more persons pursuing essential goals. Most, if not all, of the literature, has highlighted the antecedents and determinates of EL, mainly with a focus primarily on top management acting as an entrepreneur or as an entrepreneurial business strategist.

The entrepreneurial action most often connoted characteristics, skills, and attitudes toward organizational roles, tasks, and/or directing organizational strategies through leadership are combined as EL. There should be no confusion between entrepreneurial behavior and business entrepreneurship; as Peter Drucker (2014) advised, "An enterprise also does not need to be small and new to be an entrepreneur" (p. 22). Drucker explained that entrepreneurship is about creating and investing in something qualitatively different from what is already in existence. Entrepreneurs create new customers, new markets, and new ideas. Entrepreneurship's essence includes having a vision, forming new ventures, introducing new products, and initiating new production methods.

On the other end, Mintzberg (1989) elucidated that the entrepreneurial firm and structure are free from bureaucracies that do not allow innovation; meaning, there is a simple structure for the entrepreneurial firm. EL creates young and aggressive firms seeking new markets that pull away from status quo strategies. EL pursues strategic visions, which result from many types of experiences and human capital acquisition.[i] In sum, the entrepreneurial leaders, as such, are market error finders and market error correctors.

EL is a complex phenomenon that lies at the crossroad of many factors of a market economy and is often discussed at one or more levels of analysis (i.e., the firm, individual, or industry). EL at the individual level of analysis is evident within the firm that decides to pursue entrepreneurial patterns based on market-based realities and circumstances. Gupta, MacMillan, and Surie (2004) and many others have formulated a construct of EL contextually rooted not in the traditional entrepreneurial sense. EL can be defined as having the role of displaying optimism and confidence and integrating a shared perception to reach common goals.

Kuratko (2007) described EL as closely related to entrepreneurship with the caveat that the EL mindset "permeates the strategies of larger established organizations" (p. 5). Kuratko identified four factors of EL: vision, growth, venture performance, and strategy formulation. Fernald, Solomon, and Tarabishy (2005) asserted that entrepreneurs are seekers of opportunities, need to achieve goals, are independent-minded, take risks, and are inventive. El-Namaki (1992) defined an entrepreneurial leader as someone who has conceptual skills and conceives of instrumental ideas and is often not directly related to the organization. Roebuck (2011) described EL as using entrepreneurial behavior by finding and executing opportunities and managing changing circumstances. Similarly, Gupta et al. (2004) described EL as the "leader who can operate in a highly unpredictable world and in which competitive action inexorably and rapidly erodes whatever advantage the firm may currently enjoy" (p. 1). They described entrepreneurial leaders as those who capture the essence of what emerges in uncertain environments and, more or less, abstain from planned behaviors. Kansikas, Laakkonen, Sarpo, and Kontinen (2012) said that entrepreneurial leaders tend to be "stress-resistant, unselfconscious, assertive, nonexperimental in their actions, conscientious, conformist and competitive" (p. 141) in high-velocity environments.

Fernald et al. (2005) suggested that vision, problem-solving, decision-making, risk-taking, flexibility, and autonomy envelop the individual, entrepreneurially spirited leader's essential nature and personality. At the intersection of entrepreneurship and culture, Thurik and Wennekers (1999) explained that entrepreneurship and leadership cultivated within a society include "the attitudes and values toward work, production, wealth and saving, toward new information, invention and strangers, and finally toward risk and failure seem particularly relevant for economic growth" (p. 40). In reflection of previous studies, it is ascertainable how EL has often been unexplained concerning ACAP dependence.

However, there is merit to the notion that managers whose role is to draw on decision-making for future strategies use entrepreneurial skills. In any firm, EL can be observed as the influence of catalysts provided by individuals in a collaboration that challenges, envisions, innovates, and is strategic. In high-velocity environments, firms whose economic capabilities are used for market-based opportunities diffuse into marketplace patterns. The nature of high-velocity markets requires entrepreneurial leaders to make rapid decisions about effective firm performance (Eisenhardt, 1989).

As might be imagined, there is no concrete theory related to or descriptive of the sense that there must be a mode of propensity to action on the firm's part to enact innovative processes. In this same sense, is there a mode or propensity to innovate? There has to be an incubation period in which the firm has the capability and a structure to innovate. IP can be derived within the firm and recognized through the firm's resources and capabilities. Without the requisite capabilities, a firm cannot invest the time and energy into the risky activity of entrepreneurial decision-making that can thrust IP. Suppose the firm is willing to acquire knowledge from external sources through a merger and acquisition or otherwise. There are no guarantees that this investment of knowledge acquisition will lead to the reward of long-term patterns of innovation.

A unique factor needs further explanation—the firm's propensity to innovate. Perhaps this is a problem of standardization. Firms decide to remain on the *old system* and find that costs are too prohibitive or competitive to integrate ACAP into discovering useful IP. Does a firm with new information attempt to push the S-curve of technology or stick to the old system? In sum, the question remains: Does new knowledge shape new decisions, and do these new decisions change IP? Many theorists have examined, tested, and hypothesized various aspects of the individual entrepreneur—that is, *entrepreneurial action*. However, few have made a clear distinction between their involvement with IP or lack thereof.

Recently, a resurgence of the idea that entrepreneurial action and its connection with innovative behaviors, mostly as a booster of firm performance and driver of competitive positioning in markets, have led to entrepreneurial literature.

The very idea that leadership functions in a market system has been proclaimed (Mises, 1956) as one of the most important of any human action applied to entrepreneurship. Of course, the leadership action that would act most strongly in a competitive market is EL. Salerno (2008) explained that it is "the quality of leadership possessed by those who introduce new products or radically new methods of producing old products, the pioneers who discovered untapped markets or sources of supply" (p. 194). In this sense, the entrepreneur controls the capital and assumes the risks of using the capital employed to change conditions for one's own sake and customers' satisfaction and desires. Entrepreneurs seek ways to act in the market that reflect their purpose, skills, creativity, and ability to recombine resources based on external opportunities. How does EL as a concept work in practice? In this attempt to explain, observation of the S-curve pattern of innovation offers an exemplar showing the effects of ACAP as a reactor of time knowledge. The marketplace should be an environment where risk-taking can be maximized and rewarded for those who exhibit entrepreneurial leadership.

Innovation and Patterns

Abernathy and Utterback (1978) asked, "How does a company's innovation—and its response to innovative ideas—change as the company grows and matures?" (p. 3). There are circumstances in which a pattern associated with the internal process of ACAP should align with a company's strategic growth. When newly absorbed knowledge gets injected into the firm, the firm's gains are likely to concentrate on its units or diffuse across the firm. There is a normal tendency to combine a particular meaning when expressing entrepreneurship and innovation. It would be unwise to think of these two constructs otherwise, as innovation requires individuals to make decisions on the long-run and short-run use of resources and the best use of production factors. In this case, the level of inquiry is the transition-based pattern of innovation.

Abernathy and Utterback (1978) defined three broad IP patterns: fluid, transitional, and specific. Some internal patterns start as rigid and transition to evolutionary patterns over time. Therefore, the notion of internal IP rests on internal knowledge and capabilities and entrepreneurial organizational controls. However, patterns change due to changes in market structure, competitiveness between firms, and the successive wave the market is in at a particular time. The main thread of IP is the factors that lead up to innovation and that align with production timetables. IP has not been explicated in models and lends itself to the idea of a perpetual inflow of knowledge and rapid-fire decision-making (Cho & Linderman, 2020).

The Influence of EL on the S-Curve Pattern

The S-curve is one of the most well-known descriptive models used to explain the internal processes of introducing new technological products or novel internal processes. The S-curve displays new paradigm perspectives of older products that are overtaken by new products or processes with consideration of performance and effort. Moreover, the S-curve acknowledges the product's inherent limits once new entrants introduce new technologies or when old technologies are entered into new patterns. The current chapter examines the S-curve from a new perspective— an entrepreneurial perspective—where new knowledge is the signal that changes the slope of the S-curve and EL decision-making influences the lead and lag time of IP. That is, it is ACAP and entrepreneurial decision-making with the addition of time that, in effect, move the S-curve across the chasm.

Christensen (1992a, 1992b) posited much about the management utility of analyzing the S-cure diffusion at the firm level of analysis that serves to guide strategic decisions. Christensen highlighted four propositions that reflect the nature of EL as a primary *leaping* mechanism over the *discontinuity* phase. EL as a shifter of the S-curve has yet to be examined or discussed in current research. However, the fact remains that the firm's internal barriers affect internal change; change can inhibit a *leap* in creating a competitive advantage to attack against new entrants that are more than likely to push the frontier of new technological products and internal processes. New entrants bring new technologies to the market to compete with incumbents that are reluctant to increase their entrepreneurial behaviors and, hence, are reduced to a noncompetitive state.

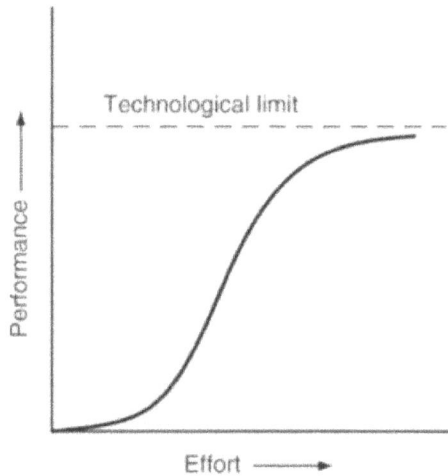

Figure 1. Technology S-curve.

The technology S-curve has been one of the hallmarks of innovation and innovative practices by firms highlighting past and present dominant designs and how it depicts the effort and performance of incumbent responses to competitive firms. The technology S-curves measure effort, performance, establishing patterns of technological advances relative to the effort needed to produce a product or technology against the tide of diminishing returns from the effort advanced. Industries change, and consumer perceptions alter throughout time. When consumer perceptions and wants change, the market alters its signals whereby firms make decisions that allow for new developments or new entrants to fill the design void. To some degree, the technology S-curve accounts for the flattening of the micro-level firm-specific S-curve product effort, performance, engineering of the product, and firm-level technological trajectory.[ii] Entrepreneurial firms understand the importance of market signals to make decisions related to innovation and product development. But what influence does the knowledge and information ELs receive have on making the S-curve move to the position of discontinuity?

Christensen (1992a) stated, "The industry's leading incumbent firms were generally the most aggressive in switching to new component technology S-curves, but there is no evidence that they gained any sort of strategic advantage over firms that stayed longer with conventional componentry" (p. 3). There are firms that, for whatever reason, do not follow the conventional steps outlined in the diffusion model itself. Firms can bypass the fermentation phase of the S-curve, and the question is how and where they received the knowledge capability to move up the S-curve and cross the chasm swiftly. Along the same lines, the technology S-curve provides context on product and industry but does not reflect the nature of high-velocity markets.

The S-curve model displays the mature aggregate product and technology pattern performance, but it is not laser-focused on the differences between a firm and its knowledge level at any place and time. The S-curve is descriptive, and it shows the effects of performance and effort related to entrepreneurial choices during a particular time frame. However, more importantly, it shows the product and technology growth and the inherently increased effort in maintaining innovation patterns. As technology becomes diffuse through markets and customers are acquainted with its use, it reaches a state of maturity, and incremental improvements may be added to form a new product, and the process of innovation (continuous or discontinuous) is a decision based on ACAP of entrepreneurial leadership.

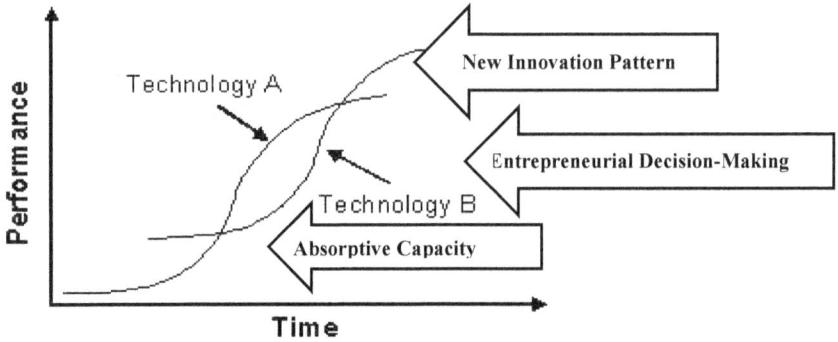

Figure 2. Technology S-curve with ACAP.

The ACAP process and EL decision-making create interfirm actions that cause shifts in the S-curve related to whether or not to consider a change of plans related to performance effort with the possibility of diminishing returns, especially in high-velocity markets. The firm's ACAP, EL, and a strong entrepreneurial orientation as internal effects might indeed be shifters of a firm's S-curve. This can be easily seen if effort and performance were replaced with knowledge and time. This assertion is definitive as the S-curve is expressed in static terms and not concerning individuals' potential to absorb knowledge as one of the motivating causes of crossing the chasm. Six propositions for future exploration include the following:

P_1:   In high-velocity markets, ACAP negatively affects a firm's entrepreneurial decisions and IP.

P_2:   In high-velocity markets, ACAP positively affects a firm's entrepreneurial decision-making and IP.

P_3:   In high-velocity markets, a firm's S-curve is altered by new ACAP.

P_4:   In high-velocity markets, a firm's newly acquired ACAP does not negatively alter IP.

P_5:   In high-velocity markets, a firm's EL decisions based on new ACAP is neutral toward IP.

P₆: In high-velocity markets, a firm's ACAP changes EL decision-making, which leads to continuous or discontinuous changes in the direction of IP.

CONCLUSION

This study poses critical questions at the intersection of ACAP processes and changes in IP influenced by EL decision-making in a given firm. This chapter provides comments to establish a research agenda in entrepreneurial theory and a new way of thinking about S-curve patterns. One factor to consider is the size of the firm. Drucker (2014) stated, "An enterprise also does not need to be small and new to be an entrepreneur." The first guiding perspective of the comments in this chapter is that EL employs human capital, which guides S-curve patterns. The second guiding perspective is that entrepreneurial leaders' decision-making toward innovation has to provide a climate that supports the emerging environment for innovation to develop.

Is EL a multifaceted construct related to the firm's knowledge acquisition and transmutation to commercializing products? Does ACAP directly influence EL within a firm in high-velocity markets? How does EL impact human capital's use and investment and the reengagement of human capital according to new market waves? Moreover, what role do entrepreneurial leaders play in firm-level innovative dynamics across the firm?

The need for creativity and innovation at the firm level has been extensively researched. There is not enough evidence in entrepreneurial and innovation literature about the dynamic nature of ACAP consequences on EL decisions and patterns of innovation. Perhaps the propensity of knowledge linked with innovation has become less critical than the realized *ex-post* innovation. While this may be the case, there is untapped gold in this vein because "it is important to distinguish between a firm's willingness or 'readiness' to innovate and the outcomes which result from this" (Klass & Wood, 2009, p. 2). However, we must integrate the propensity to innovate due to market activity with knowledge acquisition, competition, high-velocity firms, markets, and industries.

Hormiga, Hancock, and Valls-Pasola (2013) examined the propensity to innovate at the individual level—primarily human capital. There tends to be a significant agreement between Hormiga et al. and Fontana, D'Alise, and Marzano (2015), who believed, "Innovative propensity flourishes when the organisation encourages it, when employees are motivated to think and pursue new ideas, and when the organisation provides employees with the resources they need to play with these ideas in generative ways" (p. 40). Many intricate moving parts of the enterprise have an indirect and/or direct impact on a firm's ability to create and sustain innovation. However, in this case, these intricate moving parts are enveloped and integrated into a cyclical theoretical interpretation called *coiling and recoiling* effects.

The current chapter attempted to connect knowledge and the use of knowledge and the inner workings of what makes the S-curve move toward crossing the *chasm*. A firm is likely to establish IP internally, but this is assumed to be ACAP as determinate and not antecedent. Along these same lines, very few studies have acknowledged EL's role in IP in market economies and the impact on learning curves and spillover effects. This study proposed that EL decision-making intensifies entrepreneurship proclivities as well as disrupting IP.

ENDNOTES

1. Abernathy and Utterback's (1978) focused on the transition between patterns and certain conditions that manifest themselves as the internal conditions that support increased innovative technological changes. They provided examples of radical transition innovations with Texas Instruments and the electric light bulb—having gone through multiple innovative revolutions.

2. Scott Shane (2009) provided a list of firms' failures to foresee future market changes and provided six reasons why the S-curve shifts.

3. Fredrick A. von Hayek (1980) made numerous points about the individual nature of knowledge and its dispersion across many people in society in *Individualism and Economic Order*.

4. In *The Analysis of Economic Change*, J. A. Schumpeter (1935) determined there are three wave/cycle schemas: long, medium, and short. These waves/cycles are called Kondratieff cycles that last 40-60 years, Juglar cycles that last 7-11 years, and Kitchin cycles that last 0-3 years. The importance of these cycles is that they create changes in the market, moving away from equilibrium. Examples include the first wave Industrial Revolution, the second wave of steam and steel, and the third wave of electrical developments.

5. There is tacit knowledge, mundane knowledge, and technical knowledge. However, beneath these surfaces, there are no other knowledge descriptions that can be absorbed in a firm that link directly or indirectly with innovation.

6. Henry Mintzberg (1989) used an excellent example of visionary leadership when he quoted Lee Iacocca about growing up in the automobile business, where he went from Chrysler to Ford.

7. Market realities and circumstances are various elements in which the market rotates, such as new competitors, prices, and customer preference changes. This idea of market realities and circumstances relates to whether or not to innovate to keep up with the industry or if a product or service requires more resources to stay relevant to its intended customer.

8. In *The Flowering of the Third America*, Maury Klein (1993) discussed the market pertaining to entrepreneurs as being dynamic and not static. The environment must be open to a range of choices and options and should not be constrained toward new ideas when individuals pursue economic interests.

9. Christensen (1992a) mentioned the details of the S-curve theory.

10. Drucker (2014) gave examples of General Electric as being entrepreneurial in many of their product lines and credit servicing units. He also spoke of McDonald's as the epitome of entrepreneurship because they saw the *value* to customers and improved and renewed their processes and tools to generate new customers and new markets.

REFERENCES

Abernathy, W. J., & Utterback, J. M. (1978). Patterns of industrial innovation. *Technology Review, 80*(7), 40-47.

Childs, J. (2015). *Organization: Contemporary principles and practice*. Malden, MA: John Wiley & Sons.

Cho, Y. S., & Linderman, K. (2020). Resource-based product and process innovation model: Theory development and empirical validation. *Sustainability, 12*(3), 913.

Christensen, C. M. (1992a). Exploring the limits of the technology S-curve. Part I: Component technologies. *Production and Operations Management, 1*(4), 334-357.

Christensen, C. M. (1992b). Exploring the limits of the technology S-curve. Part II: Architectural technologies. *Production and Operations Management, 1*(4), 358-366.

Cohen, W. M., & Levinthal, D. A. (1990). Absorptive capacity: A new perspective on learning and innovation. *Administrative Science Quarterly*, 128-152.

Den Hertog, P., & Bilderbeek, R. (1999, March). *Conceptualising service innovation and service innovation patterns*. Research Programme Strategic Information Provision on Innovation in Services (SIID) for the Ministry of Economic Affairs, Directorate for General Technology Policy. Retrieved from http://citeseerx.ist.psu.edu/viewdoc/download?doi=10.1.1.10 2.9390&rep=rep1&type=pdf

Drucker, P. (2014). *Innovation and entrepreneurship*. New York, NY: Routledge.

Eisenhardt, K. M. (1989). Making fast strategic decisions in high-velocity environments. *Academy of Management Journal, 32*(3), 543-576.

Eisenhardt, K. M., & Martin, J. A. (2000). Dynamic capabilities: What are they? *Strategic Management Journal, 21*(10-11), 1105-1121.

El-Namaki, M. S. S. (1992). Creating a corporate vision. *Long Range Planning, 25*(6), 25-29.

Fernald, L. W., Solomon, G. T., & Tarabishy, A. (2005). A new paradigm: Entrepreneurial leadership. *Southern Business Review, 30*(2), 1-10.

Fontana, F., D'Alise, C., & Marzano, M. A. (2015). Incentives and innovative propensity. *Review of Contemporary Business Research, 4*(2), 39-56.

Gross, R. (2017). Exploring the moderating impact of absorptive capacity on strategic thinking, innovative behavior, and entrepreneurial orientation at the organizational level of analysis. *Journal of Management Policy and Practice, 18*(3), 60-73.

Gross, R. (2018). Exploring the influence of slack resources and absorptive capacity on strategic flexibility using the Miles and Snow taxonomy: A review and future research agenda. *Journal of Applied Business & Economics, 20*(5). https://doi.org/10.33423/jabe.v20i5.363

Gupta, V., MacMillan, I. C., & Surie, G. (2004). Entrepreneurial leadership: Developing and measuring a cross-cultural construct. *Journal of Business Venturing, 19*(2), 241-260.

Hayek, F. A. (1945). The use of knowledge in society. *The American Economic Review, 35*(4), 519-530.

Hayek, F. A. (1980). *Individualism and economic order.* Chicago, IL: University of Chicago Press.

Hormiga, E., Hancock, C., & Valls-Pasola, J. (2013). The relationship between employee propensity to innovate and their decision to create a company. *Management Decision, 51*(5), 938-953.

Kansikas, J., Laakkonen, A., Sarpo, V., & Kontinen, T. (2012). Entrepreneurial leadership and families as resources for strategic entrepreneurship. *International Journal of Entrepreneurial Behavior & Research, 18*(2), 141-158. https://doi.org/10.1108/13552551211204193

Klass, D., & Wood, M. (2009). Propensity to innovate: Driving innovation in a professional services firm. *Journal of Construction Engineering and Management,* 146(3), 1-24.

Klein, M. (1993). *The flowering of the third America: The making of an organizational society, 1850-1920.* Chicago, IL: Ivan R Dee.

Kuratko, D. F. (2007). Entrepreneurial leadership in the 21st century: Guest editor's perspective. *Journal of Leadership & Organizational Studies, 13*(4), 1-11.

Lindsey, P. H., & Norman, D. A. (1977). *Human information processing: An introduction to psychology.* New York, NY: Academic Press.

Menger, C. (2007). *Principles of Economics.* Auburn, AL: Ludwig von Mises Institute.

Mintzberg, H. (1989). *Mintzberg on management: Inside our strange world of organizations.* New York, NY: Simon and Schuster.

Mises, L. V. (1956). *Human action* (Scholar's ed.). Auburn, AL: Mises Institute.

Oliver, J. J. (2012). Winning in high-velocity markets: The case of BSkyB. *Strategic Direction, 28*(10), 3-5. doi:http://dx.doi.org.pfeiffer.idm.oclc.org/10.1108/02580541 211268366

Oliver, J. J. (2016). High-velocity markets drive adaptive capabilities. *Strategic Direction, 32*(1), 5-7. doi:http://dx.doi.org.pfeiffer.idm.oclc.org/10.1108/SD-07-2015-0111

Rai, R. K. (2011). Knowledge management and organizational culture: A theoretical integrative framework. *Journal of Knowledge Management, 15*(5), 779-801. doi:http://dx.doi.org.pfeiffer.idm.oclc.org/10.1108/13673271 111174320

Roebuck, C. (2011). *Critical need for entrepreneurial leaders during turbulent times.* Retrieved from Transforming Organisational & Individual Performance via Entrepreneurial Leadership website: http://chrisroebuck. co/blog/critical-need-for-entrepreneurial-leadersduring-turbulent-times

Salerno, J. T. (2008). The entrepreneur: Real and imagined. *The Quarterly Journal of Austrian Economics, 11*(3-4), 188-207.

Schumpeter, J. A. (1934). *The theory of economic development.* New Brunswick, NJ: Transaction.

Schumpeter, J. A. (1935). The analysis of economic change. *The Review of Economics and Statistics, 17*(4), 2-10.

Schumpeter, J. A. (1964). *Business cycles: A theoretical, historical and statistical analysis of the capitalist process* (Abridged, with an introduction by Rendigs Fels). Philadelphia, PA: McGraw-Hill.

Shane, S. (2009). *Technology strategy for managers and entrepreneurs.* Upper Saddle River, NJ: Pearson Education.

Srikanth, J., & Mohanavel, S. (2017, December). *High-velocity enterprises–A strategic perspective.* Retrieved from https://www.researchgate.net/publication/322063549_High_ Velocity_Enterprises-A_Strategic_Perspective

Thurik, R., & Wennekers, S. (1999). Linking entrepreneurship and economic growth. *Small Business Economics, 13*(1), 27-56.

Wirtz, B. W., Mathieu, A., & Schilke, O. (2007). Strategy in high-velocity environments. *Long Range Planning, 40*(3), 295-313.

Chapter 8:
Innovative Behavior and Strategic Thinking

This chapter presents a frontier analysis, linking two previously separate constructs that cut across many organizational functions: innovative behavior and strategic thinking. Strategic thinking is often viewed, prima facie, as a dynamic capability and used as a competitive apparatus. The factors that influence this mode of thinking have rarely been questioned.

This study advances theory by examining the effect of innovative behavior on strategic thinking from the organizational perspective. The final analysis suggests that innovative behavior positively and significantly impacts individuals and teams' strategic thinking.

INTRODUCTION

Innovative behavior can positively and negatively affect an organization's climate, process, and structure. Some of the more familiar of these are co-worker stress, strategic direction, and control over workload, perception of management, and management support. In a business landscape with vigilant competitors, management is charged with leading with an entrepreneurial spirit; this spirit is transmitted to employees, affecting others' behaviors and thinking. If management cultivates innovative behavior, then innovative behavior might affect strategic thinking capabilities. This research uses an interactionist perspective (Janssen, 2005) to explore the interaction between ideation and employee behavior in innovative pursuits in the workplace. Therefore, this research examines the impact (or lack thereof) of innovative behavior on employees' strategic thinking. It also explicates the linkages between innovative behavior and strategic thinking and whether the two are antecedent or determinant of managerial and employee-level strategic thinking.

The literature review describes the effects of innovative behavior and the risk involved in the transmutation of ideas and outlines the personal factors related to the potential socio-political outcomes (Dougherty & Heller, 1994; Janssen, 2005) when innovative behavior is unleashed in a constrained organizational system. This notion is apparent in the work of Gross (2016), who implied that strategic thinking "is dependent on the firm's social system, as the strategic thinkers can incorporate, motivate and find support within systems that can both cultivate and encourage this mode of thinking" (p. 34).

Henceforth, there are structural and psychological implications to implementing strategic thinking and innovative behavior; conversely, the interaction of these variables has significant bearings on the outcomes of employees' behavioral decisions. Flora Hung (2004) agreed that there is a constrained view of this behavior despite either innovative approach (social or individual). The social structure determines the outcomes of innovative behaviors. From

Flora Hung's perspective, there is evidence that external to the organizational ecosystem, market demands are related to an organization's propensity to embrace and cultivate innovative behavior.

Organizations' competitive positioning in the business landscape forces managers to face many innovative challenges. Opportunities, resource allocation, and realized and potential capabilities require organization members to use strategic thinking to increase internal levels of absorptive capacity. If organizational members can think strategically about how and when to disrupt their markets, then they can compete, sustain themselves, and endure in a market position over time. However, there has been teasing out of the differences between strategic thinking and other cognitive theories in management studies.

Capra (2002) focused on process thinking, March and Simon (1958) brought forth the development and use of cognitive mapping, and Senge (1990) viewed thinking at the level of the firm as a social system and as a process. Basadur, Runco, and Vega (2000) discussed the role of creative thinking, and Gross (2016) described leadership styles as reinforcement of managerial, strategic thinking. While strategic thinking contains many elements of the cognitive processes, other modes of thinking do not use the same attributes of thinking that were presented in Liedtka's (1998) five pillars of strategic thinking and Norzailan, Yusaf, and Othman's (2016) strategic competencies (Gross, 2016). Nuntamanop, Kauranen, and Igel (2013) are correct in seeing a gap between strategic thinking and strategic management.

Smith and Tushman (2005) maintained that for firms to survive and remain competitive, management must capitalize on short-term efficiency and insist on innovative long-term strategies. In such a system, emerging behavior is rooted in a firm's stock of knowledge at any point in time allows for flexibility in a firm's pursuit of an organizational strategy. Taking the psychological empowerment perspective, according to Pieterse, van Knippenberg, Schippers, and Stam (2010), individuals who are actively engaged in their work role have the motivation (Thomas & Velthouse, 1990) and self-efficacy to be empowered to make emerging decisions. However, strategic thinking's embedded focus makes this proposition more sound, effective, and opportune in today's organization. The crux of this assertion might assist in making innovative behavior a primary antecedent of strategic thinking.

Herein, the interplay is explored between behavior and thinking, where both intersect to form the manifestations of novel ideas and adaption of new tools and technologies to compete. With this line of thought, this intersection broadens the external purview so that competitors are acknowledged along with their potential capabilities, and potential internal capabilities can be defused and transmuted into realized capabilities (Cohen & Levinthal, 1990) to meet market dynamics and competitive forces in real time (Smith & Tushman, 2005). This research examines the interaction between innovative behavior as the independent variable and strategic thinking as the dependent variable. The research hypothesis is *that innovative behavior positively impacts individual strategic thinking in an organizational context.* This research is framed with a review of the literature, discussion, and a conclusion. This chapter presents the literature on innovative behavior and strategic thinking within the context of the firm.

LITERATURE REVIEW

A Panoramic View of Innovative Behavior

Innovative behavior can be traced to Robertson's (1967) seminal work in which innovation was categorized as continuous, dynamically continuous, and discontinuous. All three have a disruptive nature. Innovation is disruptive both in markets and within the organizational structure. Innovative behavior has four dimensions: idea exploration, idea generation, idea championing, and idea implementation (De Jong & Den Hartog, 2007; Janssen, 2005; Scott & Bruce, 1994; West & Farr, 1989).

Following the landmark study by Scott and Bruce (1994), distinctions were made between creativity, innovative behavior, and their effects on organizational climate. Although both terms have a connotation of novelty, newness, and adaption, innovative behavior encompasses both the generation and implementation of ideas that exist on a continuum (Scott & Bruce, 1994; West & Farr, 1990). Janssen (2005) explained that innovative behavior can be realized in the firm and has both perceived and actual effects on individuals' ability to conceive and implement ideas, primarily social arrangements in the workplace that establish appropriate behaviors among members and innovative behavior are a challenge to workplace norms (Ford, 1996; Janssen, 2005).

Wu, Parker, and de Jong (2014) proposed that in employees who engage in higher levels of work-related cognition, their activities are related to innovative behavior. Wu et al. concluded that people who need high levels of work-related cognitive activity seek novel ideas and tend to engage in complicated and psychologically risky ideas. Wu et al.'s research included 179 employees between 22-64 years of age with job tenure ranging from 2-40 years. They argued that employees with a high need for cognition in their work-task were more likely to develop stronger attitudes about the novelty of discovery and process ideas. Consistent with their hypothesis, employees with a strong need for cognition engage more than those with less, even when moderated by job pressure and deadlines.

Innovative behavior and its perceived influences on employee inputs can improve many efficiencies and productivity indicators, including increased organizational performance and a stronger relationship between employees and suppliers and/or customers. In this sense, innovative behavior is a creative and value-enhancing engagement (Drazin, Glynn, & Kazajian, 1999). Whether the engagement produces novelty or not, it is the unrelenting innovative orientation of individuals involved in the sense-making of errors and a perception of a better use of held resources. The outcomes have implications for the group, team, and organizational levels of analysis (Greenberg, 1990). Taking a process-oriented approach to innovative behavior does not always fit neatly into organizational systems based on the pivotal role and interaction with management objectives and the sociopolitical milieu in organizational systems.

Janssen (2005) collected samples from 187 employees who were not managers, using hierarchical regression and controlling for gender, age, and job tenure. Janssen suggested that employee-perceived influence and supervisor support of innovative behavior were positively related to innovative behavior. When employees believe they impact a process, they engage in behaviors that require creativity on their part as a personal investment in the said creative process. In contrast, if employees perceive that their supervisor disapproves of subordinates' ideas, they will be less likely to engage in innovative behavior.

Learning organizations outperform those that do not embrace new knowledge and do not use knowledge to develop and cultivate tools that would confer an advantage in process and product/service development. The core elements of the learning organization are leadership, organizational support, encouragement, and employee development, and consist of two dimensions: people and structure (Park, Song, Yoon, & Kim, 2014). Park et al. (2014) found connections between learning organizations, managerial innovative behavior, and absorptive capacity (Cohen & Levinthal, 1990), where knowledge acquired (internally or externally) thus filters through organizational processes based on structural acquisition, assimilation to exploitation, and commercialization of the acquired knowledge. Park et al. concluded that work engagement mediates the relationship between learning organizations and innovative behavior.

If organizational learning is to permeate the organization ecosystem, it needs a climate conducive to autonomy, collaboration, and support (Ren & Zhang, 2015). When the organizational climate is strong, employees are committed to the innovative process, which involves learning and applying new knowledge. The organizational climate is critical for the sociopolitical and psychological effects of supporting innovative behavior in the workplace. Ren and Zhang (2015) found a significant correlation between organizational climate and innovation on innovative employee behavior; job challenges and stressors did not moderate the relationship between strategic thinking and innovative behavior to make a large enough effect.

H₁: Innovative behavior has a positive impact on individual strategic thinking in an organizational context.

A Latitudinal View of Strategic Thinking

Pisapia, Ellington, Toussaint, and Morris (2011) presented three dimensions of strategic thinking: reframing, reflection, and systems thinking. Reframing is the ability to think through multiple lenses, even during the chaos. One must change perceptions based on situations and changing simultaneously their previously held perspectives, particularly when implementing novel ideas. Overall, one has to reflect, examine, and reexamine both success and failures in light of historical events, along with consideration of currently held assumptions concerning rules, policies, and procedures. Pisapia et al. stated that strategic thinking "requires the ability to recognize patterns, examine new possibilities, dealing with large chunks of information, and the ability to pull pieces together into a big picture" (p. 2).

Bonn (2005) postulated that strategic thinking solves problems inherent in strategy, where one culls both rational and convergent thought processes. With technological advances in the workplace and the competitive forces in the dynamic business landscape, management and employees alike must possess strategic thinking skills and competencies. Regardless of the cognitive and environmental contextual factors discussed in the literature, it is *axiomatic* that strategic thinkers' use remains imperative in dynamic industries. Those with an *unconstrained* view of strategic thinking (Bonn, 2005; Heracleous, 1998; Liedtka, 1998) approve of its use in creative, analytical, and visionary capabilities that lay *outside* the scope of traditional boundaries of the social structure. However, there is a *constrained* view of strategic thinking (Keeney, 1994) where values are placed in lockstep with action derived from principled and conventional preemptive identification based on decision-making.

Organizational leaders can use foresight to prepare for any unforeseen events. When a strategy fails unexpectedly, strategic thinking can support the need for realignment (Self, Self, Matuszek, & Schraeder, 2015). If derailment results from employee and management inertia, misdirection, or lack of leadership, this reverberates throughout the organization. Jelenc, Pisapia, and Ivancic (2016) found that strategic thinking is positively linked with entrepreneurial attitude orientation; there was a direct link with innovation, one of the entrepreneurial attitude orientation domains.

Strategic thinking has been documented by many theorists (Allio, 2012; Gross, 2016; Haycock, 2012; Nuntamanop et al., 2013; Pisapia et al., 2011) and found to be significantly and positively related to transformational and transactional leadership styles (Gross, 2016). Of the three leadership styles, both transformational and transactional were significant and positively related to strategic thinking; laissez-faire was not. Strategic thinking must be viewed in terms of its effects on individuals' ability within the ecosystem and on the paradigm of management and leadership (Gross, 2016). However, leaders' mind maps and models need to be transformed, redefined, and reinterpreted in order to transmute innovative ideas, attitudes, and behaviors linked to increased strategic thinking at the organizational level.

Managers with a *parochial* view of strategy might find themselves working under an old paradigm that is incompatible with the new institutional demands based on new stocks of knowledge. Many contextual factors are tied to hypercompetitive markets, fast developments, and knowledge sharing through open innovation methodologies. This causes an unconstrained view of strategic thinking that makes critical decisions and adjustments in real time. With the consistent practice of strategic thinking, it is easy to believe that the more an action is repeated, the better one gets at it. Consistent practice and exposure to various tasks and projects would accumulate into a reservoir from which one could draw when thinking strategically.

Dragoni, Oh, Vankatwyk, and Tesluk (2011) sampled 700 executives to test whether work experience accumulation was related to strategic thinking. They used hierarchical regression analysis, controlling for gender, ethnicity, and work experience and found that accumulated work experience impacted strategic thinking and cognitive ability in dealing with organizational demands for change and market demands; however, this finding does not aid in causation. Goldman (2012) suggested leadership practices to enhance organizational members' strategic thinking. Because strategic thinking is embedded in organizational culture, organizational leadership is paramount in its cultivation and execution (Gross, 2016). Goldman and Casey (2010) discerned three conceptualizations of strategic thinking concerning organizational culture:

1. Strategic thinking is essential to strategy development.

2. Strategic thinking is a mental/cognitive process.

3. Strategic thinking involves perspectives and social activities.

Goldman (2012) suggested that organizational leaders have to create more cognitive and social interaction through leadership skills to enhance strategic thinking empowerment linked to individual performance. The leadership practices of the executive-level respondents in this study were either heavy or light as to whether they were able to increase strategic thinking in the front-line and middle ranks of management. These leadership practices are relevant when managers discuss and review external changes with organizational members and how those changes might affect, for example, their (a) current or future situations, (b) need to allocate resources and alternate strategy planning roles, (c) need to recognize individual/team strategic thinkers, and (d) need to formulate organizational policies and procedures that contribute to resolving crises.

DISCUSSION

This juncture opens new theoretical windows that further inquiries can now explore. Innovative behavior and its dimensions can be effective if a sustainable culture within the organizational structure and management has adopted a systems view (Liedtka, 1998). Organizational members can apply and engage in innovative behavior in work-related tasks. On the same note, thinking-in-time and hypothesis-driven skills are linked with the dimensions of innovative behavior (e.g., idea generation, idea implementation, idea champion, and idea exploration). To think in time, one must generate and concretize ideas; a person who is hypothesis-driven has the cognitive ability to explore and test ideas in real time.

The finding in this research aligns well with the outcomes of Carmeli, Meitar, and Weisberg (2006) who positively linked behavior with constructive thought strategies and individual behavior and individuals' intrinsic abilities. Carmeli et al. showed that individuals' predictive patterns of innovative behavior and engagement are perceived as self-assertion and self-leadership skills, either needed or possessed, to establish more substantial innovative behavior in their job roles. Martins and Terblanche's (2003) cultural perspective seems consistent with this finding of the direct relation of leadership, engagement, culture, and strategic thinking, and individual innovative behavior. They surmised that culture is at the core of innovation and strategy and that there needs to be greater emphasis on quantifying the interaction among these variables.

CONCLUSION

This research brings a new theoretical development to the innovative behavior and strategic thinking literature by suggesting a significant and positive impact of innovative behavior on individual strategic thinking. This study should be used as a proxy and baseline for future developments linking other organizational and managerial constructs to strategic thinking and making, building, and alignment a firm's overall strategy and strategic reference points.

Now that this study has been linked, its practical implications are warranted. Organizational leaders should enhance the connections between innovative behavior with the conceptualization of strategic thinking and the implementation of ideas to encourage active strategic thinking. The implementation of new and valuable ideas fosters a change of perspective, reframing abilities that increase one's view of systems. The notion that idea exploration, generation, implementation, and championing precedes the benefits of strategic thinking is critical. Although this study is parochial in many respects, managers can draw important implications that concretize the full spectrum of idea exploration and effects on employee strategic thinking.

The psychological effects of this behavior are buttressed by employees' perception of management supportiveness and institutional flexibility. Formulating ideas, devising strategy, and realigning tactics can be onerous; however, this development views strategic engagement and planning and the value of idea generation fostered by non-managers and managers alike. Strategic thinking considers multiple frames and strategies and is antithetical to an organizational *constrained* view and should be viewed as a perceptual process.

REFERENCES

Allio, R. J. (2012). Leaders and leadership–Many theories, but what advice is reliable? *Strategy & Leadership*, *41*(1), 4-14. https://doi.org/10.1108/10878571311290016

Basadur, M., Runco, M. A., & Vega, L. A. (2000). Understanding how creative thinking skills, attitudes and behaviors work together: A causal process model. *The Journal of* Creative *Behavior*, *34*(2), 77-100. https://doi.org/10.1002/j.21626057.2000.tb01203.x

Bonn, I. (2005). Improving strategic thinking: A multilevel approach. *Leadership & Organization Development Journal, 26*(5), 336-354. https://doi.org/10.1108/01437730510607844

Capra, F. (2002). *The hidden connections: A science for sustainable living.* New York, NY: Harper Collins.

Carmeli, A., Meitar, R., & Weisberg, J. (2006). Self-leadership skills and innovative behavior at work. *International Journal of Manpower, 27*(1), 75-90. https://doi.org/10.1108/01437720610652853

Cohen, W. M., & Levinthal, D. A. (1990). Absorptive capacity: A new perspective on learning and innovation. *Administrative Science Quarterly, 35*(1), 128-152. https://doi.org/10.1016/B978-0-7506-7223-8.50005-8

De Jong, J. P., & Den Hartog, D. N. (2007). How leaders influence employees' innovative behaviour. *European Journal of Innovation Management, 10*(1), 41-64. https://doi.org/10.1108/14601060710720546

Dougherty, D., & Heller, T. (1994). The illegitimacy of successful product innovation in established firms. *Organization Science, 5*(2), 200-218. https://doi.org/10.1287/orsc.5.2.200

Dragoni, L., Oh, I. S., Vankatwyk, P., & Tesluk, P. E. (2011). Developing executive leaders: The relative contribution of cognitive ability, personality, and the accumulation of work experience in predicting strategic thinking competency. *Personnel Psychology, 64*(4), 829-864. https://doi.org/10.1111/j.17446570.2011.01229.x

Drazin, R., Glynn, M. A., & Kazanjian, R. K. (1999). Multilevel theorizing about creativity in organizations: A sensemaking perspective. *Academy of Management Review, 24*(2), 286-307. https://doi.org/10.5465/amr.1999.1893937

Flora Hung, C. J. (2004). Cultural influence on relationship cultivation strategies: Multinational companies in China. *Journal of Communication Management, 8*(3), 264-281. https://doi.org/10.1108/13632540410807682

Ford, C. M. (1996). A theory of individual creative action in multiple social domains. *Academy of Management Review,*

21(4), 1112-1142.
https://doi.org/10.5465/amr.1996.9704071865

Goldman, E. F. (2012). Leadership practices that encourage strategic thinking. *Journal of Strategy and Management, 5*(1), 25-40. https://doi.org/10.1108/17554251211200437

Goldman, E. F., & Casey, A. (2010). Building a culture that encourages strategic thinking. *Journal of Leadership & Organizational Studies, 17*(2), 119-128. https://doi.org/10.1177/1548051810369677

Greenberg, J. (1990). Organizational justice: Yesterday, today, and tomorrow. *Journal of Management, 16*(2), 399-432. https://doi.org/10.1177/014920639001600208

Gross, R. (2016). Towards an understanding of the relationship between leadership styles and strategic thinking: A small and medium enterprise perspective. *Journal of Business Studies Quarterly, 8*(2), 22-39.

Haycock, K. (2012). Strategic thinking and leadership. *Library Leadership & Management, 26*(3/4).

Heracleous, L. (1998). Strategic thinking or strategic planning? *Long Range Planning, 31*(3), 481-487. https://doi.org/10.1016/S0024-6301(98)80015-0

Janssen, O. (2005). The joint impact of perceived influence and supervisor supportiveness on employee innovative behaviour. *Journal of Occupational and Organizational Psychology, 78*(4), 573-579. https://doi.org/10.1348/096317905X25823

Jelenc, L., Pisapia, J., & Ivancic, V. (2016). *Strategic thinking capability and entrepreneurial attitude orientation: Links and relations.* Retrieved from https://www.researchgate.net/publication/303920645_Strate gic_Thinking_Capab ility_and_Entrepreneurial_Attitude_Orientation_Links_and_ Relations

Keeney, R. L. (1994). Creativity in decision making with value-focused thinking. *Sloan Management Review, 35*(4), 33.

Liedtka, J. M. (1998). Strategic thinking: can it be taught? *Long Range Planning, 31*(1), 120-129. https://doi.org/10.1016/S0024-6301(97)00098-8

March, J. G., & Simon, H. A. (1958). *Organizations.* Oxford, England: Wiley.

Martins, E. C., & Terblanche, F. (2003). Building organisational culture that stimulates creativity and innovation. *European Journal of Innovation Management, 6*(1), 64-74. https://doi.org/10.1108/14601060310456337

Norzailan, Z., Yusof, S. M., & Othman, R. (2016). Developing strategic leadership competencies. *Journal of Advanced Management Science, 4*(1), 66-71.

Nuntamanop, P., Kauranen, I., & Igel, B. (2013). A new model of strategic thinking competency. *Journal of Strategy and Management, 6*(3), 242-264. https://doi.org/10.1108/JSMA-10-2012-0052

Park, Y. K., Song, J. H., Yoon, S. W., & Kim, J. (2014). Learning organization and innovative behavior: The mediating effect of work engagement. *European Journal of Training and Development, 38*(1/2), 75-94. https://doi.org/10.1108/EJTD-04-2013-0040

Pieterse, A. N., Van Knippenberg, D., Schippers, M., & Stam, D. (2010). Transformational and transactional leadership and innovative behavior: The moderating role of psychological empowerment. *Journal of Organizational Behavior, 31*(4), 609-623. https://doi.org/10.1002/job.650

Pisapia, J., Ellington, L., Toussaint, G., & Morris, J. D. (2011). *Strategic thinking skills: Validation and confirmation of constructs.* Retrieved from http://fau.academia.edu/JohnPisapia/Papers/776012/Strategic_Thinking_Skills_V alidation_and_Confirmation_of_Constructs

Ren, F., & Zhang, J. (2015). Job stressors, organizational innovation climate, and employees' innovative behavior. *Creativity Research Journal, 27*(1), 16-23. https://doi.org/10.1080/10400419.2015.992659

Robertson, T. S. (1967). The process of innovation and the diffusion of innovation. *The Journal of Marketing, 31*(1), 14-19.

Scott, S. G., & Bruce, R. A. (1994). Determinants of innovative behavior: A path model of individual innovation in the workplace. *Academy of Management Journal, 37*(3), 580-607. https://doi.org/10.5465/256701

Self, D. R., Self, T., Matuszek, T., & Schraeder, M. (2015). Improving organizational alignment by enhancing strategic thinking. *Development and Learning in Organizations: An International Journal, 29*(1), 11-14. https://doi.org/10.1108/DLO-08-2013-0053

Senge, P. M. (1990). *The fifth discipline.* New York, NY: Doubleday/Currency.

Smith, W. K., & Tushman, M. L. (2005). Managing strategic contradictions: A top management model for managing innovation streams. *Organization Science, 16*(5), 522-536. https://doi.org/10.1287/orsc.1050.0134

Thomas, K. W., & Velthouse, B. A. (1990). Cognitive elements of empowerment: An "interpretive" model of intrinsic task motivation. *Academy of Management Review, 15*(4), 666-681. https://doi.org/10.5465/amr.1990.4310926

West, M. A., & Farr, J. L. (1989). Innovation at work: Psychological perspectives. *Social Behavior, 4*(1),15-30.

West, M. A., & Farr, J. L. (1990). *innovation and creativity at work: Psychological and organizational strategies.* New York, NY: John Wiley & Sons.

Wu, C. H., Parker, S. K., & De Jong, J. P. (2014). Need for cognition as an antecedent of individual innovation behavior. *Journal of Management, 40*(6), 1511-1534. https://doi.org/10.1177/0149206311429862

Chapter 9:
Leadership Styles and Strategic Thinking

This chapter examines leadership styles' relationship with strategic thinking in small- and medium-sized enterprises (SMEs), which is an area that has yet to be explored. The research expands conventional thought regarding the role of leadership styles on employees' strategic thinking. This approach is significant because it serves as a presbyopia baseline study for the continuation of knowledge in the construct of strategic thinking and leadership theory in the SME.

This avenue of examination suggests that transformational and transactional leadership styles significantly impact employee strategic thinking. Moreover, the laissez-faire leadership style shows to be linked to individual strategic thinking. Practical and theoretical implications are provided as well as future research areas.

INTRODUCTION

Research on strategic orientation is generally (Aloulou & Fayolle, 2005; Hakala, 2011; Salavou et al., 2004) limited, mainly related to the development of strategy in the entrepreneurial context (Kazmi & Naaranoja, 2013, p. 44). Zahra, Sapienza, and Per Davidson (2006) claimed, "Most research and theory building has focused on established companies, thus ignoring new ventures and SMEs" (p. 4). Performance is vitally important to SME survival; however, it is equally important to examine what drives employee strategic thinking in the workplace—the kind of strategic thinking that translates to action and maintains competitive advantages for the firm. Research studies related to strategy, leadership styles, and SMEs are sparse and do not provide the theoretical support showing the effects of leadership styles nor elements of strategic thinking at the crossroad.

O'Regan, Ghobadian, and Sims (2004) echoed this very sentiment: "Most of the studies to date have focused on examining the bilateral relationship between two of these variables in a single study, rather than examining the relationship between variables simultaneously" (p. 46). They further stated, "The majority of the literature focuses on large firms, and there is a dearth of research on smaller organizations" (p. 45). The primary research question asks: Is there a leadership style related to employee strategic thinking? The secondary question asks: Which of the leadership styles are significant in strategic thinking? To examine these relationships, robust statistical analysis is used to investigate these potential relationships. Employees' innovative, entrepreneurial, and strategic thinking have been understudied in their relationship with leadership styles. There is a need for quantifiable justification for the interaction between these variables (Gross, 2016).

Gross (2016) focused on a similar area of inquiry, which showed a positive relationship between transformational and transactional styles with entrepreneurial and innovative behaviors in Indian immigrant and American firms (Gross & Cabanda, 2016). However, there is still a need for more quantitative testing with this construct to explore the relationships and predictive nature with other organizational functions and behaviors. Understanding entrepreneurial leaders' styles and cognitive capabilities in shaping vision and direction and employing appropriate framing based on immediate and spontaneous unforeseen situations are contemporary and salient issues in extant literature. The following sections present the research hypotheses, literature review, conclusion, implications, practical implications, Theoretical Implications, and future research.

The research hypotheses follow:

H_1: Transformational leadership style has a positive relationship with strategic thinking.

H_2: Transactional leadership style has a positive relationship with strategic thinking.

H_3: Laissez-faire leadership style has a negative relationship with strategic thinking.

This research is framed by leadership styles and strategic thinking and is described using literature that pertains to each of the presented independent and dependent variables. Literature included in this review were selected and added to the proceeding section based on the research approach and analyses conducted; that is, each of the included research studies was quantitative.

LITERATUVE REVIEW

Leaders' behaviors are observable to subordinates through their verbal and nonverbal actions and communications with employees and co-managers, giving the observer cues as to their leadership style. As subordinates observe leaders' behaviors, there is a counter outcome behavior of the employee, which makes leader style essential and complex. As such, leadership styles comprise three distinct variations of behaviors, each with explicit visions of how leaders seek to influence their groups, teams, and individuals in their firm to meet commonly held goals.

Yukl (2009) explained that leadership is the act of guiding, facilitating, and influencing followers during activities related to the organization. Therefore, leadership styles are patterns and approaches used to influence subordinate outcome behaviors that fit the demands of the SME environment or the leader's vision. Because there is no one way to lead employees, SME leaders could essentially employ different styles to engage different subordinates based on their needs or situations. The presented leadership style topology is broken into three unique approaches: transformational, transactional, and laissez-faire.

Burns (1978) introduced the conceptualization of transactional and transformational leadership based on a political perspective. The difference between transactional and transformational styles is primarily based on the medium of exchange between leaders and followers. Transformational leaders focus on higher-order exchanges that involve deeper long-term relationships with followers. Transactional leaders identify the needs of employees, reconcile their needs with those of others, and then attempt to provide the need exchange based on resources. Bass (1985) concluded that transformational and transactional leadership embody similar behaviors; however, conceptually, the two styles are different as these differences are apparent in their dimensions. Although each style is distinct, leaders use different elements of each style because no one style can be used in all situations. Therefore, leaders simultaneously and arbitrarily interchange styles. Over time, however, there is a consistent, observable trend toward a particular style.

A considerable amount of research has used transformational leadership as a focal point, mainly examining its effectiveness in business and organizational contexts. Burns' (1978) description of transformational leadership was that it uplifts employees' morale and motivation and supports their immediate needs and self-interests. The transformational style is intended to grow and mature subordinates and develop them in ways that allow them to do more than what they might have thought was possible themselves (Burns, 1978). Lowe, Kroeck, and Sivasubramaniam (2006) explained,

"Transformational leaders seek new ways of working, seek opportunities in the face of risk, prefer effective answers to efficient answers, and are less likely to support the status quo" (p. 3).

Transformational leadership is composed of four unique domains: idealized influence, intellectual stimulation, individual consideration, and inspirational motivation. Transformational leadership style has been tested both qualitatively and quantitatively, and the consensus is that it empowers followers to be independent, develops visions, and articulates a vision with high attention to others in a way that stimulates the intellect, and inspires people to a large degree (Lowe et al., 1996).

Aga, Noorderhaven, and Vallejo (2016) explained, "A transformational project manager motivates and inspires team members towards a holistic conception of project success, characterized by efficiency, effectiveness, and stakeholder satisfaction" (p. 814). In fact, this study used a population of 200 project development managers and found that the components of transformational leadership (i.e., idealized influence, intellectual stimulation, individual consideration, and inspirational motivation) were effective in team-based project success. These transformational domains combined, according to Aga et al., impact employee commitment, guide novel and creative ideas, and encourage the development of individual potential (Avolio, Zhu, Koh, & Bhatia, 2004).

Several studies showed that transactional leadership was positively correlated with many organizational behaviors and functions (Barling, Weber, & Kelloway, 1996). A few studies reported that transactional leadership style correlates with entrepreneurial business performance and firm growth and influences employees' strategic behavior (Bass et al., 2003; Chung-Wen, 2008; Lowe et al., 1996; Norzailan, Yusof, & Othman, 2016). The transactional style of leadership is based on identifiable and mutually beneficial transactions between followers and leaders. The transactional leader's focus is the antithesis of that of transformational leaders; the primary focus is on how to exchange resources for either compliance or performance (Judge & Piccolo, 2004).

The two domains of transactional leadership are contingent reward and active/passive management by exception (Howell & Avolio, 1993; Judge & Piccolo, 2004). Transactional leaders identify the needs of employees and provide for those needs based on resources. Bass (1985) persisted that transformational and transactional leadership embody similar behaviors; however, conceptually, the two styles are different as these differences are apparent in their outcomes. The leadership style domains are encapsulated in the behavioral approach of transactional leaders and visually observable by employees and involve exchanges ranging from praise to punishment (Antonakis, 2001; Avolio et al., 1999; Bass, 1997; Judge & Piccolo, 2004; Yukl, 2004). For example, the contingent reward is based on the "degree to which the leader sets up constructive transactions or exchanges with followers: The leader clarifies expectations and establishes the rewards for meeting these expectations" (Judge & Piccolo, 2004, p. 755).

Active management by exception is when leaders "monitor follower behavior, anticipate problems and take corrective actions before the behavior creates serious difficulties" (Judge & Piccolo, 2004, p. 755). Passive management by exception is when leaders "wait until the behavior has created problems before taking action" (Judge & Piccolo, 2004, p. 755). Wofford and Goodwin (1994) explained that transactional leaders' foci are on defined performance goals, goal commitment, role expectations, and task-related skills. This style also focuses on the task, targets, and levels of achievement. The underpinning of this leadership style is the explicit exchange between each individual involved based on mutually satisfying agreements. All exchanges made are not equivalent, as some exchanges are distinguished between low- and high-quality (Kuhnert & Lewis, 1987).

O'Regan et al. (2004) quantitatively tested leadership styles, performance attainment, and strategy. They found transactional leadership to be significantly correlated with short-term performance and to be internally oriented. Leaders who focus on short-term performance improvement initiatives used a transactional style due to the extrinsic view of the exchanges by the receiving parties. In the same vein, transactional leadership style was positively correlated with strategy as a control mechanism. Love and Roper (2015) suggested that because transactional style is correlated with control, smaller firms see benefits in managers employing a transactional style to control and monitor employee performance.

Regarding the laissez-faire leadership style, a sparse amount of research has reported on how it affects followers' behavior within the firm (Hinkin & Schriesheim, 2008). Although Gross (2016) showed that laissez-faire style positively relates with entrepreneurial orientation and negatively to innovative behavior in Indian immigrant firms, there is no knowledge as to how laissez-faire relates to strategic thinking in SMEs. Further, the laissez-faire style is often missed and overlooked and rarely focus on when examining its relationship, correlation, and impact.

This style is connoted with the term *nonleadership*, which essentially means "avoiding decisions, hesitating to take action, and being absent when needed" (Hinkin & Schriesheim, 2008. p. 4). The behaviors of laissez-faire leaders are unintentional, not premeditated, and often go unnoticed by the leaders themselves; thus, subordinates' behaviors become motivated by various internal and external environmental factors (Hinkin & Schriesheim, 2008). According to Hinkin and Schriesheim (2008), the laissez-faire style has two dimensions: *reward omission*, which is when "managers do not respond to what a subordinate perceives to be his or her good performance," and *punishment omission*, which occurs when "managers do not respond to what a subordinate perceives to be his or her poor performance" (p. 8).

Strategic thinking is a thought process conducted by individuals to creatively reinterpret the most held positions and attitudes regarding an organization's strategy. This mode of thinking is often considered as *out of the box* when, in fact, the act of strategic thinking is *within the box* and used primarily as a source to avoid derailment from a failing strategy. For example, if one employs strategic thinking to develop a strategy with management tools alone, it will not ensure success. That is, strategic thinking serves to maintain and ultimately increase competitive organizational positioning through value-added actions, which thus requires the narrowing of the gulf between echelons and reshaping the organizational social architecture to fit emerging environmental situations and new opportunities within a commonly held framework. According to Bonn (2005) who posited that strategic thinking is "the way of solving strategic problems that combines a rational and convergent approach with creative and divergent thought process" (p. 8).

Strategic thinking is an overall mindset that includes the requisite competencies and skillsets that enable one to conceptualize strategy in terms of *thinking*—thinking directly or indirectly allied to the firm's processes, situational contexts, and content. Strategic thinking is the opposite of thinking linearly or maintaining the status quo; thus, strategic thinking requires one to use systems thinking, reflection, and reframing skills (Pisapia, 2005). Pisapia, Pang, Hee, Lin, and Morris (2009) stated, "Leaders who find themselves in such messy, chaotic, complex environments fail because they are trained in and rely upon linear thinking that does not work in situations characterized by ambiguity and complexity" (p. 46).

Strategic thinking and strategic planning are different (Bonn, 2005) theoretically but interrelated by a myopic view on solving strategic problems when deployed. Strategic thinking attempts to balance the ebbs and flows of the internal and external landscape in which the firm exists and incorporate both realities back into the firm's contextual realities as a check to either deviate or stay the course of a strategic plan.

The mindset of strategic thinkers is not linear, nor do they overuse quantifiable indicators as the only navigation mechanism (Pisapia et al., 2009). This suggests that strategic thinking can activate a mental model that incorporates multidimensional and interrelated functions of the firm to drive change, create momentum, garner support, and react proactively upon the realization of untapped interfirm and intrafirm opportunity. The leader can think through problems and align thinking with emerging real-time unplanned change. Indeed, leaders have courses of action they must execute (i.e., the strategic plan). The reality is that markets are hyper-competitive and volatile, which requires leaders to think aberrantly about emerging solutions to emerging issues (Graetz, 2002).

Strategic thinking depends on the firm's social system because the strategic thinker can incorporate, motivate, and find support within systems that can both cultivate and encourage this mode of thinking. Similarly, other modes of thinking have been brought to the fore that are aligned with the broad understanding of strategic thinking, such as process thinking within the firm's system (Capra, 2002), cognitive mapping/schema thinking (March & Simon, 1958), systems thinking (Senge, 1990), creative thinking (Basadur, Runco, & Vega, 2000), and framing (Perkins, 1986).

Three strategic thinking skills were identified as being salient and fundamental for engaging vision and direction. Pisapia et al. (2009) outlined three strategic thinking dimensions: reframing, reflecting, and systems thinking. Reframing is a conscious effort to use multiple perspectives to gain deeper insight to generate new courses of action. Reflecting encompasses the ability to discern and add personal experiences to make sound judgments. Technical, practical, and critical skills comprise the reflecting stage. Systems thinking is having an awareness of one's surroundings, relationships, how one's role fits into the firm's spin wheel of functions, and how their input and output impacts the entire ecosystem.

Liedtka (1998) clearly distinguished between strategic thinking and strategic planning, explaining that strategic thinking is a concept of practice at the individual level while strategic planning operates at the firm level. Most importantly, strategic thinking is process-oriented. This thinking mode finds opportunity or a direction that is promising but is often invisible to others. Based on the five pillars of strategic thinking (Liedtka, 1998), the salient elements that comprise strategic thinking are systems perspective, intent-focused, thinking in time, hypothesis-driven, and intelligent opportunism.

The domains of strategic thinking are categorized as capabilities that can theoretically be diffused at all levels of an organization but initiate at the individual level. Goldman and Casey (2010) agreed that strategic thinking is critical for leading organizations' existing and future strategic plans. Goldman and Casey asserted, "Limited work has been done addressing individual, group, and contextual factors contributing to strategic thinking" (p. 119). The diffusion of strategic thinking has the potential to transform all levels of a firm. Although the inception is at the individual level, it ultimately needs organizational support to reach the potential of being diffused. Strategic thinking requires one to apply experience, knowledge, and hypotheses to a situation to resolve an issue. Although this style of thinking can be attributed to many internal and external factors, it is the mode that becomes activated when one's experience is reflected upon and exercised through the strategic action process, which in turn increases strategic learning. Goldman and Casey echoed Yukl (2006), who asserted, "For maximum impact, learning experiences need to include an element of challenge, provide feedback, and allow the learner to reflect on the experience and identify learning from it" (p. 125). Strategic thinking is reinforced with internal feedback, individual reflectivity, and the ability to apply it in chaotic or challenging situations within the firm.

Amitabh and Sahay (2008) proposed that strategic thinkers embody a specific set of niche attributes that distinguishes them from non-strategic thinkers. These attributes include the ability to lead, visualize long-term future scenarios, form broad-based strategies and allow others to emerge in time, look for environmental cues to develop, identify patterns based on intuitive thinking, and rewrites rules of competition. The strategic thinking attribute model echoes the importance of strategic choices and decision-making by leaders. Strategic thinkers make decisions based on current situations and can project the future impact of decisions made by other members of their firm. Essentially, the strategic thinking of firm members should circumvent a core vision. Amitabh and Sahay shared the sentiments of Ohmae (1982), who described strategic thinking within the firm as an "idiosyncratic mode of thinking in which company, customers and competition merges in a dynamic interaction out of which a comprehensive set of objectives and plans of action eventually crystallizes" (p. 6). Norzailan et al. (2016) proposed a few strategic thinking competencies essential to engage, think, and form an independent judgment effectively. These competencies accumulate as leaders mentally transition from a conceptual to operational mindset while simultaneously thinking of the potential implications of strategic tactics.

Nuntamanop, Kauranen, and Igel (2013) purported there is a "gap of knowledge in definition and attributes of strategic thinking in strategic management" (p. 248). They proposed a strategic thinking process model that includes characteristics that impact business strategy due to strategic thinking by firm leaders. The authors used the recommendation of Tovstiga (2010), who explained that the strategic thinking process includes "developing strategic questions, forming issues, developing insight using strategic analysis, assessing the competitive landscape, and generating strategic options" (p. 247). Nuntamanop et al. revealed 25 skills and abilities linked with strategic thinking. Nuntamanop et al.'s skills and abilities include conceptual thinking ability, visionary thinking, creativity, analytical thinking ability, learning ability, synthesizing ability, and objectivity. Their strategic thinking model concretizes the strategic thinking competencies. The Nuntamanop et al. model supports the notion that strategic thinking formulation is primarily conducted at the individual level. Their model analysis suggests that when business strategists use these competencies based on the elements in the competency model, they can better identify, test, and readily pursue strategic decisions. In the same vein, Waal et al. (2012) expressed that intuition plays an essential role in the effectiveness of strategic thinking, which ultimately leads to dynamic strategic formulations, actions, and strong organizational performance.

Szekely (2015) proposed the three levels of strategic thinking model adopted from Baracskai and Valencei (2011). This model purports that strategic thinking can only be as successful as its thinkers. In this view and applying the levels provided by Szekely, strategic thinking develops sequentially; eventually, through experience, skillfulness, and implementation, one can exhibit good judgment and decision-making in a time of organizational need. Strategic thinking skills, according to Szekely, add to one's ability to think creatively, innovatively, and conceptually within a frame of reference. The levels of strategic thinking function within and around organizational politics, organizational design, and organizational constraints. The first level is *how* individuals can find the right strategy by exploring the organization's strengths and weaknesses using strategic analysis; they have competencies to aggregate and reliable data to move an initiative forward. The second level is *when* individuals can use learning to perpetuate innovative techniques, implant these innovative techniques to new situations, and use innovation to solve ongoing solutions within firms. The third level explains that *when* individuals have both experiences and can augment their experience, they can fuse older and new information to create a vision and formulate a strategic direction.

CONCLUSION

Few studies have empirically tested the relationship of leadership styles on strategic thinking to date. This examination adds to the theoretical understanding of how leadership and strategy are related, but more needs to be done in this area. Both the transformational leadership style and the transactional leadership style have a positive relationship with strategic thinking. Although strategic thinking is positively related to leadership styles within the context of the firm, the laissez-faire style has a positive relationship with strategic thinking. Remember that reward omission and punishment omission together comprise the domains of laissez-faire leadership style (Hinkin & Schriesheim, 2008).

This finding is somewhat dissimilar from previous research but is along the same lines as the rather misleading notion that laissez-faire style has a negative association with positive organizational outcomes. For example, Skogstad, Einarsen, Torsheim, Aasland,

and Hetland (2007) purported that laissez-faire style predicts workplace stressors. When employees are exposed to a laissez-faire style leader, their perceptions of the leader's employee treatment quality diminish over time (Skogstad et al., 2007). The laissez-faire style was negatively associated with employee job satisfaction, negatively impactful on a group and team climate (Judge & Piccolo, 2004), and negatively associated with ethical leadership (Ofori, 2009). Consequently, most studies using laissez-faire leadership style tend to report negative associations with other organizational behaviors, but few have tested laissez-faire with a construct that requires individual initiation and cognitive processing as in this research.

Although laissez-faire did not meet significance in the third hypothesis, it showed a positive relation, which is worth mentioning. Viewing laissez-faire through the lens of Norzailan et al.'s (2016) strategic thinking competencies, Liedtka's (1998) pillars of strategic thinking, and Pisapia et al.'s (2009) strategic thinking, reflection, and reframing strategic dimensions, it makes sense that laissez-faire had a positive relationship with strategic thinking; these dimensions, competencies, and pillars incorporate elements of self-initiation, reflection, and awareness. Therefore, it is conceivable that laissez-faire style, if increased, would be related to an increase in strategic thinking due to the individual nature of strategic thinking.

Based on the positive and statistically significant relationship, transactional and transformational styles both provide theoretical and practical direction for future research; that is, entrepreneurial leaders can employ styles to direct and sustain entrepreneurism. Conceptually, what can be suggested is that the transformational style embodies elements that support strategic thinking. The transformational domains of individual consideration, intellectual stimulation, idealized influence, and inspirational motivation present strong linkage with the competencies of strategic thinking proposed by Norzailan et al. (2016), such as providing deliberate practice, reflective learning, and creation of experience density.

Further, transactional leadership was positively related to strategic thinking as the domains of the transactional style, especially contingent reward, could be the main influencing factor in this finding. Lowe et al. (1996), Bass et al. (2003), Chung-Wen (2008), and Norzailan et al. (2016) showed contingent reward to be correlated with business performance, growth, and a powerful influence in motiving employees. Strategic thinking is aimed at growth potential and increased performance, making sense of the competitive environment; albeit this mode of thinking is initiated at the individual level, it is shared among the broader social context of the firm.

The positive link among transformational leadership, transactional leadership, and strategic thinking suggests that because strategic thinking is related to leadership styles, leaders can assist and cultivate strategic thinking behaviors so that employees can better position themselves to deal with unplanned change (Graetz, 2002). Szekely (2015) added that strategic thinkers could handle strategy deviation because they think of the *why, what, how,* and *when* in each situation, consider resources, and efficiently use timing to create the best solution. These thought elements are positively related to contingent reward, management by exception, intellectual stimulation, idealized influence, and individual consideration, which, coupled with strategic thinking processes, helps strategic thinkers create new paths by framing and mind mapping new unforeseen opportunities.

Amitabh and Sahay (2008) added a dynamic interaction among strategic thinking, the firm, and its customers. This dynamism results from the internal creation of tacit knowledge, which is the outgrowth of strategic thinking. This assertion is in line with the results of the findings in this research as Pérez-Luño, Saparito, and Gopalakrishnan (2016) also found that high levels of entrepreneurism is positively correlated with the use and creation of tacit knowledge; internally transferable knowledge can be used and harnessed, allowing strategic thinkers to employ it deliberately.

IMPLICATIONS

Leadership styles employed to support and cultivate employee strategic thinking capabilities have intended and unintended consequences. This research does not support the assumption that strategic thinking is initiated due to management leadership per se; rather, it is a process that can be cultivated and utilized by employees in supporting the goals of the firm. Therefore, the net balance of strategic thinking is strong when entrepreneurial leaders exhibit certain styles that are significant and strong. Strategic thinking involves a process-orientation whereby knowledge is gained and then strategically used (Pérez-Luño et al., 2016) to find the best solution or trade-off from a set of choices considering the available resources (Szekely, 2015). However, there must be support at the firm level where the infrastructure is designed for strategic thinkers to impact. According to Norzailan et al. (2016), leader managers and entrepreneurs should develop integrated and non-substitutable effective strategic thinking competencies. In this case, there are both practical and theoretical implications that leaders, managers, and entrepreneurs should consider.

Practical Implications

In a practical sense, entrepreneurial leaders use many variations of leading interchangeably, depending on current and preexisting situations. However, one style may have more currency power than another. Lowe et al. (1996) suggested this view and contended that transformational leadership is the antithesis of the status quo; transformational leadership is, to a large degree, used to seek opportunities, face risk, invest in relationships and grow others. Transactional style, on the contrary, seeks to provide exchanges that entice others so they can focus on the firm's goals and targets and reaching higher levels of achievement. Therefore, the effect of these styles on strategic thinking is paramount and a strong mechanism to increase performance. Managers who employ exchanges to focus employees on goal attainment can work for the short term. However, effective strategic thinking requires gathering information, using the information, and implementing the information to halt management inertia or complacency. Strategic thinking represents a movement away from firm inertia and complacency. Nuntamanop et al. (2013) explained that firms should have a structure where managers with leadership capabilities can co-develop employees in terms of conceptual thinking ability, visionary thinking, creativity, analytical thinking ability, learning ability, and synthesizing ability.

Theoretical Implications

In a theoretical sense, the literature on strategic thinking has not been tested empirically with leadership theories; therefore, the nature and correlation of strategic thinking with other leadership behaviors are essentially nonexistent (O'Regan et al., 2004). Similarly, not much progress has been made on a theoretical basis between strategic thinking and strategic planning (Bonn, 2005) in strategic literature; however, it seems this is changing. Research has shown that strategic thinking is linked with individual entrepreneurial behavior (Jelenc & Pisapia, 2015), impacting upper echelon decision-making and influencing the firm's social system (Capra, 2002), and is influential among cultural elements and cultural distance (Dragoni et al., 2014). These findings provide a baseline in bridging the gulf between strategic thinking and leadership theory through sound quantitative analysis to thrust future research forward. This allows strategic thinking to be tested across the plethora of leadership models, constructs, and theories such that researchers can actualize a causal relation with leadership and gain a more substantial theoretical basis in understanding the antecedents of managerial, strategic thinking in the process of leading members in a firm, group, or team.

FUTURE RESEARCH

Future inquiries on strategic thinking should focus on teams and workgroups and the impact of leaders' behaviors on geographically dispersed teams. This should include a focus on strategic thinking in teams with an added cultural component, where various cultures focus on how strategic thinking is viewed, rewarded, and supported within the various functions of the firm—large or small.

There should also be more quantitative testing of strategic thinking competencies related to SME efficiency, productivity, and absorptive capacity. Future research could capitalize on a narrower industry that could provide more insights on how strategic thinking is rewarded, motivated, and pursued compared with other industries or cultures. The same is true with leadership: perhaps leadership styles react somewhat differently when tested in a specific industry and within a different larger context.

REFERENCES

Aga, D. A., Noorderhaven, N., & Vallejo, B. (2016). Transformational leadership and project success: The mediating role of team-building. *International Journal of Project Management, 34*(5), 806-818.

Aloulou, W., & Fayolle, A. (2005). A conceptual approach of entrepreneurial orientation within small business context. *Journal of Enterprising Culture, 13*(01), 21-45.

Amitabh, M., & Sahay, A. (2008, May). *Strategic thinking: Is leadership the missing link: An exploratory study.* Paper presented at the 11th Annual Conversation of the Strategic Management Forum, Kanpur, India.

Antonakis, J. (2001). The validity of the transformational, transactional, and laissez-faire leadership model as measured by the Multifactor Leadership Questionnaire (MLQ 5X). Unpublished doctoral dissertation, Walden University, Minneapolis, MN.

Avolio, B. J. (1999). Full leadership development: Building the vital forces in organizations. Thousand Oaks, CA: Sage.

Avolio, B. J., Zhu, W., Koh, W., & Bhatia, P. (2004). Transformational leadership and organizational commitment: Mediating role of psychological empowerment and moderating role of structural distance. *Journal of Organizational Behavior, 25*(8), 951-968.

Baracskai, Z., Velencei, J., Dörfler, V., & Szendrey, J. (2011). Designing a 'Strategic Partner' School. *IABE 2011 Las Vegas: International Academy of Business and Economics.*

Barling, J., Weber, T., & Kelloway, E. K. (1996). Effects of transformational leadership training on attitudinal and financial outcomes: A field experiment. *Journal of Applied Psychology, 81*(6), 827.

Basadur, M. I. N., Runco, M. A., & Vega, L. A. (2000). Understanding how creative thinking skills, attitudes and behaviors work together: A causal process model. *The Journal of Creative Behavior, 34*(2), 77-100.

Bass, B. M. (1985). Leadership and performance beyond expectations. New York: Free Press.

Bass, B. M. (1997). Does the transactional–transformational leadership paradigm transcend organizational and national boundaries?. *American Psychologist, 52*(2), 130.

Bass, B. M., Avolio, B. J., Jung, D. I., & Berson, Y. (2003). Predicting unit performance by assessing transformational and transactional leadership. *Journal of applied psychology, 88*(2), 207.

Bonn, I. (2005). Improving strategic thinking: a multilevel approach. *Leadership & Organization Development Journal.*

Burns, J. M. G. (1978). *Leadership.* New York, NY: Harper & Row.

Capra, F. (2002). The Hidden Connections, Doubleday, New York, NY.

Chung-Wen, Y. (2008). The relationships among leadership styles, entrepreneurial orientation, and business performance. *Managing Global Transitions, 6*(3), 257.

De Waal, G. A., & Knott, P. (2012). Product innovation tool adoption behaviour in technology-based new ventures. *International Journal of Innovation Management, 16*(03), 1240001.

Dragoni, L., Oh, I. S., Tesluk, P. E., Moore, O. A., VanKatwyk, P., & Hazucha, J. (2014). Developing leaders' strategic thinking through global work experience: The moderating role of cultural distance. *Journal of Applied Psychology, 99*(5), 867.

Goldman, E. F., & Casey, A. (2010). Building a culture that encourages strategic thinking. *Journal of Leadership & Organizational Studies, 17*(2), 119-128.

Graetz, F. (2002). Strategic thinking versus strategic planning: Towards understanding the complementarities. *Management Decision, 40*(5), 456-462.

Gross, R. (2015). Situational interview method as a predictor of strategic thinking: A theoretical framework. *Global Business and Economics Research Journal, 4*(1), 1-16.

Gross, R. (2016). *The impact of leadership styles on employee entrepreneurial orientation and innovative behavior: A comparative analysis of American and Indian immigrant entrepreneurs* (Doctoral dissertation, Regent University). Retrieved from http://search.proquest.com/openview/ded1f395860c0208ebfc faceaebedf6d/1?pq-origsite=gscholar&cbl=18750&diss=y

Gross, R., & Cabanda, E. (2016). Modelling the relationship between leadership styles and innovative behavior and entrepreneurial orientation in American firms. *Review of Business and Technology Research, 13*(1), 1-7.

Hakala, H. (2011). Strategic orientations in management literature: Three approaches to understanding the interaction between market, technology, entrepreneurial and learning orientations. *International Journal of Management Reviews, 13*(2), 199-217.

Hinkin, T. R., & Schriesheim, C. A. (2008). An examination of "nonleadership": From laissez-faire leadership to leader reward omission and punishment omission. *Journal of Applied Psychology, 93*(6), 12-34.

Howell, J. M., & Avolio, B. J. (1993). Transformational leadership, transactional leadership, locus of control, and support for innovation: Key predictors of consolidated-business-unit performance. *Journal of applied psychology, 78*(6), 891.

Jelenc, L., & Pisapia, J. (2015). Individual entrepreneurial behavior in Croatian IT firms: The contribution of strategic thinking skills. *Journal of Information and Organizational Sciences, 39*(2), 163-182.

Judge, T. A., & Piccolo, R. F. (2004). Transformational and transactional leadership: A meta-analytic test of their relative validity. *Journal of Applied Psychology, 89*(5), 755.

Kazmi, S. A. Z., & Naaranoja, M. (2013). Connecting individual differences in workforce to organizational creativity through transformational leadership for corporate transformational effectiveness! *Open Journal of Leadership, 2*(04), 73.

Kuhnert, K. W., & Lewis, P. (1987). Transactional and transformational leadership: A constructive/developmental analysis. *Academy of Management Review, 12*(4), 648-657.

Liedtka, J. M. (1998). Strategic thinking: Can it be taught? *Long Range Planning, 31*(1), 120-129.

Love, J. H., & Roper, S. (2015). SME innovation, exporting and growth: A review of existing evidence. *International Small Business Journal, 33*(1), 28-48.

Lowe, K. B., Kroeck, K. G., & Sivasubramaniam, N. (1996). Effectiveness correlates of transformational and transactional leadership: A meta-analytic review of the MLQ literature. *The Leadership Quarterly, 7*(3), 385-425.

March, J. G., & Simon, H. A. (1958). *Organizations.* Oxford, England: Wiley.

Norzailan, Z., Yusof, S. M., & Othman, R. (2016). Developing strategic leadership competencies. *Journal of Advanced Management Science, 4*(1), 66-71.

Nuntamanop, P., Kauranen, I., & Igel, B. (2013). A new model of strategic thinking competency. *Journal of Strategy and Management, 6*(3), 242-264. https://doi.org/10.1108/JSMA-10-2012-0052

Ofori, G. (2009). Ethical leadership: Examining the relationships with full range leadership model, employee outcomes, and organizational culture. *Journal of Business Ethics, 90*(4), 533-547.

Ohmae, K. (1982). The strategic triangle: A new perspective on business unit strategy. *European Management Journal, 1*(1), 38-48.

O'Regan, N., Ghobadian, A., & Sims, M. (2004). The link between leadership, strategy, and performance in manufacturing SMEs. *Journal of Small Business Strategy, 15*(2), 45.

Pérez-Luño, A., Saparito, P., & Gopalakrishnan, S. (2016). Small and medium-sized enterprise's entrepreneurial versus market orientation and the creation of tacit knowledge. *Journal of small business management, 54*(1), 262-278.

Perkins, D. N. (1986). Thinking frames. *Educational Leadership, 43*(8), 4-10.

Pisapia, J., Reyes-Guerra, D., & Coukos-Semmel, E. (2005). Developing the leader's strategic mindset: Establishing the measures. Leadership Review, 5(1), 41-68.

Pisapia, J., Pang, N. S. K., Hee, T. F., Lin, Y., & Morris, J. D. (2009). A comparison of the use of strategic thinking skills of aspiring school leaders in Hong Kong, Malaysia, Shanghai, and the United States: An exploratory study. *International Education Studies, 2*(2), 46.

Salavou, H., Baltas, G. and Lioukas, S. (2004), "Organisational innovation in SMEs: The importance of strategic orientation and competitive structure", *European Journal of Marketing*, Vol. 38 No. 9/10, pp. 1091-1112. https://doi.org/10.1108/03090560410548889

Senge, P.M. (1990), The Fifth Discipline, Doubleday/Currency, New York

Skogstad, A., Einarsen, S., Torsheim, T., Aasland, M. S., & Hetland, H. (2007). The destructiveness of laissez-faire leadership behavior. *Journal of Occupational Health Psychology, 12*(1), 80.

Tovstiga, G. (2010) *Innovation as a dynamic capability: strategic implications and impact.* In: Strategic Management Society (SMS) 30th Annual International Conference, 12-15 Sep 2010, Rome, Italy.

Tovstiga, G. (2010). Innovation as a dynamic capability: strategic implications and impact.

Wofford, J. C., & Goodwin, V. L. (1994). A cognitive interpretation of transactional and transformational leadership theories. *The Leadership Quarterly, 5*(2), 161-186.

Yukl, G., & Lepsinger, R. (2004). *Flexible leadership: Creating value by balancing multiple challenges and choices* (Vol. 223). John Wiley & Sons.

Yukl, G. A., & Becker, W. S. (2006). Effective empowerment in organizations. *Organization Management Journal, 3*(3), 210-231.

Yukl, G. (2009). Leading organizational learning: Reflections on theory and research. *The Leadership Quarterly, 20*(1), 49-53.

Zahra, S. A., H. J. Sapienza and P. Davidson (2006). 'Entrepreneurship and dynamic capabilities: a review, model and research agen connaissances est un processus